DEMOCRATIC REPUBLIC OF CONGO
in Pictures

Francesca Davis DiPiazza

Twenty-First Century Books

Contents

Twenty-First Century Books
A division of Lerner Publishing Group, Inc.
241 First Avenue North
Minneapolis, MN 55401 U.S.A.

Website address: www.lernerbooks.com

web enhanced @ www.vgsbooks.com

Library of Congress Cataloging-in-Publication Data

DiPiazza, Francesca, 1961–
        Democratic Republic of Congo in pictures / by Francesca Davis DiPiazza.
            p.   cm. — (Visual geography series)
        Includes bibliographical references and index.
        ISBN 978-0-8225-8572-5 (lib. bdg. : alk. paper)
            1. Congo (Democratic Republic)—Juvenile literature. 2. Congo (Democratic Republic)—Pictorial works—
    Juvenile literature. I. Title.
    DT644.D57 2008
    967.51—dc22   2007022062

Manufactured in the United States of America
1 2 3 4 5 6 - PA - 13 12 11 10 09 08

INTRODUCTION

The Democratic Republic of Congo is a county of astonishing diversity in central Africa. The nation's estimated 63 million people belong to more than two hundred ethnic groups. Congo is home to more kinds of plants and animals than almost anywhere else on Earth. Tropical rain forests cover one-third of the country. Africa's second-largest river, the mighty Congo, cuts through thick forest. Diamonds, gold, and timber are among the land's rich natural resources. A history of colonialism, corrupt politics, and violence has cast long shadows over the country, however, and modern Congo is one of the world's poorest nations.

People have lived in Congo for more than ten thousand years. The first settlers survived by hunting animals and gathering wild plants in the rain forest. By A.D. 800, different groups of Bantu-speaking peoples had migrated from western Africa and lived throughout Congo. They forged metals into tools, weapons, and ornaments.

From the fifteenth to the late nineteenth centuries, many separate kingdoms evolved in Congo. Most people lived in villages. They got their food by farming, hunting, and fishing. The arts and religion—including mask making, dancing, and storytelling—played a central role in their lives. In the sixteenth century, slave raiders began to attack Congo villages. They captured villagers and sold them into slavery. Most ended up as slaves in the Americas.

In 1884 a new kind of exploitation began in Congo. That year King Leopold II of Belgium claimed the Congo Free State as his own private property. His agents forced Congolese people to work for no pay. The agents' extreme methods caused misery and death for millions, while Leopold became wealthy from selling Congo's valuable rubber and ivory. An international outcry led Belgian lawmakers to take over the Congo Free State in 1908. They renamed the colony the Belgian Congo.

Belgians oversaw the building of some schools, hospitals, and roads. They introduced French, one of the languages of Belgium, to Congo. But everyday life for the Congolese changed little. The colonial rulers did not consider Africans fit to govern themselves and gave

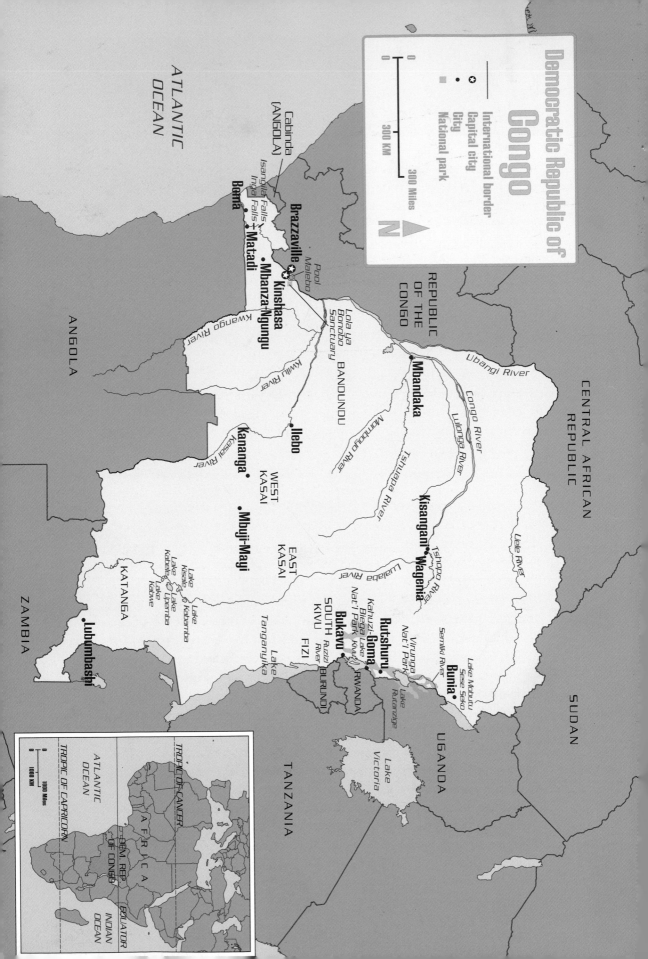

Democratic Republic of
Congo

International border
Capital city
City
National park

0
0
300 KM
300 Miles

N

ATLANTIC
OCEAN

CENTRAL AFRICAN
REPUBLIC

REPUBLIC
OF THE
CONGO

Cabinda
(ANGOLA)

Isangila Falls
Inga Falls

Boma

Brazzaville

Matadi

Mbanza-Ngungu

Kinshasa

Pool
Maleba

Kwango River

Kwilu River

Lola ya
Bonobo
Sanctuary

BANDUNDU

Mombolo River

Ilebo

Kananga

Kasai River

WEST
KASAI

Mbuji-Mayi

EAST
KASAI

Mbandaka

Ubangi River

Congo River

Lulonga River

Tshuapa River

Uele River

Semliki River

Kisangani
Wagenia

Tshopo River

Lualaba River

Lake Mobutu
Sese Seko

Lake
Rutanzige

Bunia

UGANDA

Rutshuru
Virunga
Nat'l Park

Goma

Kahuzi-
Biega Lake Kivu
Nat'l Park
Bukavu

SOUTH
KIVU

Ruzizi
River

RWANDA

BURUNDI

FIZI

Lake
Victoria

Lake
Tanganyika

ANGOLA

KATANGA

Lake
Kisale & Kabamba
Lake
Kabele
Lake
Upemba
Lake
Kabwe

ZAMBIA

Lubumbashi

TANZANIA

ATLANTIC
OCEAN

TROPIC OF CANCER

A F R I C A

DEM. REP.
OF CONGO

EQUATOR

TROPIC OF CAPRICORN

INDIAN
OCEAN

0
0
1000 KM
1000 Miles

SUDAN

Congo's people little say in the colonial government. During the 1950s, the Congolese demanded independence from Belgian rule. Talks led to a free Democratic Republic of Congo (DRC) on June 30, 1960.

Civil conflicts soon broke out in the new nation. In 1961 political rivals killed Congo's prime minister. By 1965 the head of the army, Mobutu Sese Seko, had taken over the country. He renamed it Zaire.

Congo's former names are Congo Free State (1885–1908), Belgian Congo (1908–1960), Democratic Republic of Congo (1960–1971), and Zaire (1971–1997). In 1997 its name again became Democratic Republic of Congo. The short versions of the name are DRC, Congo, or Congo-Kinshasa, after its capital city, to differentiate it from the neighboring Republic of the Congo or Congo-Brazzaville.

Using brutality and rigged elections, Mobutu held onto his power for more than thirty years. He stole billions of dollars of the nation's money and steadily worsened Zaire's standard of living. Roads fell into ruin. Little health care was available for Zaireans suffering from AIDS and other diseases. Other countries sent aid to ease the people's extreme poverty. Frequently, however, the money went into the pockets of corrupt officials.

Ethnic slaughter across the border in Rwanda in 1994 created a flood of refugees into Zaire. The influx sparked ethnic strife, which flamed into civil war in 1996. One year later, rebel leader Laurent Kabila overthrew Mobutu, ending what was later called the First Congo War (1996–1997). He restored the country's name to DRC.

The next year, rebels challenged Kabila. Several African countries joined the struggle for control of Congo. Again a civil war broke out, called the Second Congo War (1998–2003). In 2001 an assassin killed Kabila. Power passed to his son Joseph Kabila, who helped to bring peace to most of the country by 2003. The vicious five-year war killed almost 3.5 million people, either through fighting, disease, or starvation. Lawlessness and violence continued in Congo, especially in the east, where rebel militias (armed groups) still fight for power and resources.

In 2006 Congo held democratic elections after four decades of dictatorship and destruction. Voters chose Joseph Kabila as president, but fighting between supporters of opposing parties marred the election.

Amidst many divisions, music is one of the few things that unifies Congo. Fans often regard their musicians as national heroes. Influential singers such as Tabu Ley Rochereau use their popularity to promote their fellow citizens' desire for peace. After years of conflict, most Congolese people simply seek to rebuild their country.

THE LAND

Congo is the third-largest African nation, after Sudan and Algeria. With 905,063 square miles (2,344,102 square kilometers), Congo is almost one-third the size of the United States. The equator runs through northern Congo. It marks the halfway point between the North Pole and the South Pole. Nations near the equator are among the hottest places on Earth.

Congo shares boundaries with nine countries, the Atlantic Ocean, and one territory. Starting on the west and moving clockwise, Congo's neighboring countries are the Republic of the Congo (Congo-Brazzaville), Central African Republic (CAR), Sudan, Uganda, Rwanda, Burundi, Tanzania, Zambia, and Angola. North of Angola is Congo's 25-mile (40 km) Atlantic coast, where the Congo River enters the ocean. The small Angolan territory of Cabinda sits north of the coast.

⊙ Topography

Congo's four major geographical regions reflect the variety of central Africa's landscapes. The Congo Basin stretches across the northern and central parts of the country. The Northern Uplands, the Southern Uplands, and the Eastern Highlands cover the remaining land and nearly surround the basin.

The low-lying Congo Basin spans one-third of the nation's territory. The region is often called the *cuvette*—which means "basin" in French, one of the nation's official languages. The equator cuts the region almost in half. This area receives some of the heaviest annual rainfall in the world. Temperatures in the cuvette are also very high, and dense rain forest dominates the region. The huge Ituri Forest is one such rain forest. In the cuvette, most of the nutrients in the soil go into the lush forest vegetation. Therefore, the soil is not suitable for large-scale farms, and the region supports only a few farms and a sparse population.

The elevated Northern Uplands form a narrow band along the northern border of Congo. Savannas—grasslands with scattered trees—cover most of the region. The average elevation is 1,640 feet (500 meters) but rises to heights of 2,500 feet (762 m) in the northeast.

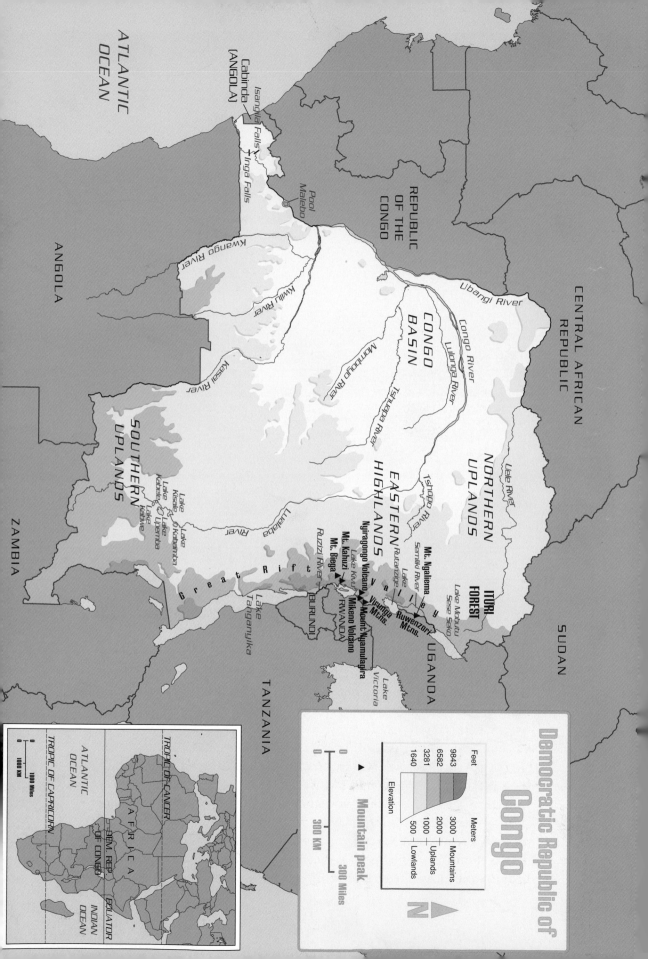

Democratic Republic of Congo

ATLANTIC OCEAN

CENTRAL AFRICAN REPUBLIC

REPUBLIC OF THE CONGO

Cabinda (ANGOLA)

ANGOLA

ZAMBIA

SUDAN

UGANDA

TANZANIA

BURUNDI

RWANDA

Isangila Falls

Inga Falls

Pool Malebo

Kwango River

Kwilu River

Kasai River

Lulonga River

Congo River

Ubangi River

Uele River

Mombuyo River

Tshuapa River

Luilaba River

Tshopo River

CONGO BASIN

NORTHERN UPLANDS

EASTERN HIGHLANDS

SOUTHERN UPLANDS

Great Rift Valley

Rift Valley

ITURI FOREST

Lake Mobutu Sese Seko

Mt. Ngaliema

Semliki River

Ruwenzori Mtns.

Lake Ruwenzori

Virunga Mtns.

Rutanzige

Njiragongo Volcano

Mikeno Volcano

Mount Nyamulagira

Lake Kivu

Mt. Kahuzi

Mt. Biega

Ruzizi River

Lake Tanganyika

Lake Victoria

Lake Kisale

Lake Kabele

Lake Kabamba

Lake Upemba

Lake Kabwe

Elevation

Feet	Meters	
9843	3000	Mountains
6582	2000	Mountains
3281	1000	Uplands
1640	500	Lowlands
0	0	Lowlands

▲ Mountain peak

300 KM

300 Miles

N

ATLANTIC OCEAN

TROPIC OF CANCER

TROPIC OF CAPRICORN

EQUATOR

AFRICA

DEM. REP. OF CONGO

INDIAN OCEAN

1000 KM

1000 Miles

Savannas and woodlands also cover the high, flat Southern Uplands, which begin south of the Congo Basin. With an average altitude of 2,730 feet (832 m) above sea level, these high plains have changing seasons. They are cooler and drier than the cuvette. The climate and soil allow local people to grow grains, such as corn and millet, and to raise cattle. Within the Southern Uplands is the Katanga (formerly Shaba) region. It contains many of Congo's mineral deposits.

Congo's Ituri Forest is almost as big as New York State. An average of 75 inches (190 cm) of rain falls in the forest yearly, mostly in heavy downpours. Humidity is almost always near 100 percent. With an average temperature of 88°F (31°C), the air is warm and sticky. However, the tall, broad-leaved evergreen trees shade the forest from direct sunlight. The forest floor stays cool and moist.

The Eastern Highlands extend 950 miles (1,529 km) southward from Lake Mobutu Sese Seko (also called Lake Albert) to the southernmost edge of the Katanga region. The highlands lie along an arm of the Great Rift Valley. The valley is a long, deep trench that stretches from the Middle East to southeastern Africa. Thick forests and grasslands cover the region. The Eastern Highlands' fertile farmland is densely populated.

A rugged series of high plateaus and mountain ranges, the Eastern Highlands reach the highest altitude in Congo. The region's tallest mountain group is the Ruwenzori. It crosses the equator south of Lake Mobutu Sese Seko. The highest peak in the range is snowcapped Margherita Peak on Mount Ngaliema (also called Mount Stanley). It rises to 16,762 feet (5,110 m).

South of the Ruwenzori are the Virunga Mountains, which include active volcanoes. Of the eight main volcanoes in the range, Mount Nyamulagira is the most active. It spews lava, smoke, and fire every three to four years.

▶ Rivers and Lakes

The 2,900-mile-long (4,640 km) Congo River is the second-longest river in Africa, after the Nile. The river forms gradually. Streams flowing out of the Eastern Highlands combine to make the Lualaba River. West of the city of Kisangani, the Lualaba becomes the Congo. As it travels westward, other rivers join and swell the volume of the Congo. At the Congolese capital of Kinshasa, 200 miles (320 km) inland from the Atlantic Ocean, the river widens into the Pool Malebo. The pool is

The **Congo River** waters Congo's lush rain forests.

actually a 50-mile-long (80 km) lake. After exiting the lake, the Congo continues westward to empty into the Atlantic Ocean.

Boats can navigate about 1,860 miles (2,993 km) of the Congo River. High waterfalls and dangerous rapids make transportation impossible on some sections. The major navigable branches of the Congo are the Kasai, Tshuapa, and Ubangi rivers. The Ubangi forms the boundary between Congo and countries to the west and north.

Congo's largest lakes are in the Eastern Highlands. These lakes serve as recreational areas and as major transportation routes between Congo and eastern Africa. Less busy are Katanga's plateau lakes. They are the remains of an inland sea that covered Congo millions of years ago. These bodies of water include Lakes Kisale, Kabwe, Kabele, Kabamba, and Upemba.

Lake Tanganyika is a 415-mile-long (668 km) body of water between Congo and Tanzania. It is the world's second-deepest lake, after Lake Baikal in Russia. The Ruzizi River connects Lake Tanganyika to Lake Kivu, which is 62 miles (99 km) long. Farther north, the Semliki River links Lake Rutanzige (also called Lake Edward) and Lake Mobutu Sese Seko. Streams from both lakes eventually flow into the Nile River.

Climate

Congo experiences a variety of climates. North of the equator, a dry season occurs from early November to late March, with very little or no rain. That same period is the rainy season in parts of the country south of the equator. The rest of the year is the rainy season. This general pattern varies, however.

Yearly rainfall ranges from 40 to 80 inches (101 to 203 centimeters) or more in Congo. The heaviest amount falls in the west and in the cuvette. Rain pours down there almost every day of the rainy season. Parts of southern Katanga, on the other hand, experience occasional droughts, or extended periods of little or no rainfall.

Temperature and humidity (moisture in the air) remain high year-round in most of Congo. Being south of the equator, Kinshasa's seasons are the reverse of those in the Northern Hemisphere. Summer temperatures in the capital city average 79°F (26°C) in January. Winters are only slightly cooler, with a July daily average of 73°F (23°C). The hottest weather occurs in the equatorial forests. Daytime readings there average about 90°F (32°C). Nighttime temperatures rarely fall below 70°F (21°C). Seasonal variations exist in the Southern Uplands, particularly in southeastern Katanga. There, cool, dry winters and warm, wet summers are the rule.

A mild, moist climate prevails in the Eastern Highlands. The average temperature is 64°F (18°C). Seasonal temperature variations in the region are slight. Humidity is high in the mountains and increases with elevation. Mists hide many of the tall slopes throughout the year. The highest mountain peaks in the east and south receive considerable snowfall.

◎ Flora and Fauna

Year-round, ample sunlight, warmth, and rain create the perfect conditions for tropical rain forests. The dense rain forest that covers one-third of Congo is among the least explored areas on Earth. It is one of the largest and thickest forests in the world. Only the small groups of people who live in the forest know many of its secrets.

At least ten thousand kinds of flowering plants grow in Congo's rain forest. Tree leaves form a canopy so

Congolese villagers work in the shadow of **Mikeno Volcano.** The volcano is part of the Virunga mountain chain.

dense that sunlight can't reach the forest floor. A wide variety of hardwood trees—such as the mahogany, ebony, iroko, black mubangu, and tola—thrive. Loggers harvest some of the trees for export, but much of the woodlands are untouched.

Trees of the Eastern Highlands include eucalyptus and pine. Europeans brought both species to the region. Dense bamboo forests grow at elevations above 6,800 feet (2,073 m). Higher still grow lobelias, briars, lichens, and orchids. These plants can survive cooler conditions. In southern Katanga, squat baobab trees grow branches that look like wild hair. The trees' thick bark protects them from drying out during the area's long dry season.

Palm trees and aloe plants grow throughout the country. Trees that yield copal resin—used in varnishes or plastics—frequently reach more than 100 feet (30 m) in height. Vines often climb up and cover them. Rubber in Congo comes from the sap of certain large vines that flourish in the jungle. Mangrove trees spread their clawlike, partly aboveground roots in marshy areas and along riverbanks.

Congo's wildlife is as varied as its vegetation. Wild animals live in areas of Congo with little population as well as in the nation's national parks. Virunga National Park is Congo's biggest and Africa's oldest wildlife reserve. Rare mountain gorillas live in the park. Less than seven hundred of these shy apes remain on Earth, and about 60 percent of them live in Congo.

A family of **mountain gorillas** eats insects from a piece of tree bark.

An **electric catfish** eats a fish after shocking it.

A SHOCKING CATCH

Villagers along Congo's rivers rely on fish as one source of food. They are happy to catch electric catfish in their nets. The edible fish grow as big as 3 feet (1 m) long and can weigh more than 40 pounds (18 kilograms). Fishers handle this fish with care while it's alive. These freshwater catfish use a special part of their bodies called an electric organ to produce an electric shock of up to 350 volts. The fish electrically stuns other fish so it can catch and eat them. It also shocks people and other animals to protect itself.

Chimpanzees and other kinds of apes, including the unusual black-and-white colobus, also live in Congo's forests. The bonobo is a great ape that lives only in Congo. Though they are also called pygmy (miniature) chimpanzees, bonobos are almost as big as their chimpanzee relatives. Adult bonobos weigh an average of 75 to 100 pounds (34 to 45 kg).

The country is home to buffalo, lions, leopards, jackals, rhinoceroses, hyenas, and baboons and other monkeys. Thousands of hippopotamuses and elephants roam vast grasslands near rivers. Smaller African forest elephants live in the jungle.

Hoofed animals include zebras, eland, and antelopes. The okapi lives nowhere else in the world except the Ituri Forest. This relative of the giraffe looks like a mix of a horse, a zebra, and a donkey. It is Congo's national animal.

Reptiles and amphibians abound in Congo. They include many kinds of snakes, such as pythons, vipers, and tree cobras. Crocodiles are common in Congo's rivers. Lizards, chameleons, salamanders, frogs, and turtles are widespread.

Congo's waters teem with a variety of fish, such as capitaine (also called Nile perch), catfish, electric fish, eels, and many others. Jellyfish live in Lake Tanganyika. Atlantic Ocean waters are home to many fish as well as whales and dolphins.

The nation's many bird species include parrots, peacocks, sunbirds, weavers, storks, eagles, and cranes. The honeyguide bird feeds on honeycomb and bee larva. People and honey badgers follow the honeyguide, which leads them to beehives.

DIAMONDS

Congo's diamonds sparkle in engagement and wedding rings around the world. As part of power tools, they also cut metal and drill into teeth. Diamonds are not only brilliant, they are Earth's hardest, longest-lasting minerals. And Congo is the world's leading supplier of industrial diamonds. Workers shape industrial diamonds into accurate cutting, boring, and grinding tools. Finely crushed diamonds, for instance, coat drill bits used by some dentists.

During Congo's recent civil wars, diamonds were part of the spiral of conflict. Warring forces illegally mined and traded diamonds and used money from their sale to buy weapons. Gems plundered in war zones are called blood diamonds or conflict diamonds.

Industrial diamonds often come in shades of yellow or brown. These rough diamonds came from a Congolese mine.

Congo's insect life is bounteous. It includes bees and beetles of many kinds, different types of grasshoppers and caterpillars, praying mantises, dragonflies, termites, ants, and centipedes. Disease-carrying tsetse flies and anopheles mosquitoes breed in warm, wet areas. Hundreds of kinds of butterflies add color to the air.

◯ Natural Resources

Congo has a wealth of natural resources. Minerals lead the list of moneymaking resources. Diamonds are Congo's most important export. Large copper deposits exist in the Katanga region, and Congo is one of the world's leading copper suppliers. Oil companies mine oil fields off the country's small Atlantic coast. Miners also exploit reserves of cobalt, cadmium, uranium, tin, silver, and gold. The mineral coltan has become important in modern times, as it is used in making cell phones.

Congo's rivers are important transportation routes. Dams and other structures harness the power of rushing water to produce electricity. The Congo River has the potential to produce much more hydropower than it does. Forest trees provide timber, rubber, and medicines, such as quinine, which treats the tropical disease malaria.

Environmental Issues

Eight reserves cover 15 percent of the nation's land and help protect Congo's abundant wildlife and plants. The government has not had the money or workers to fully patrol the parks. Extinction threatens 116 of Congo's animal species and 55 plant species. Poachers (illegal hunters) have nearly wiped out Congo's elephant population. They kill these animals for their ivory tusks, which are exported to make ivory statues, jewelry, and handicrafts.

The Discovery Channel listed being a Congo wildlife park ranger as one of the most dangerous jobs in the world. Poachers, smugglers, and armed rebels who want to control Congo's eastern borders have killed about 120 rangers since 1994. In summer 2007, rebels of the Mai Mai militia attacked park-ranger posts in the Virunga National Park. They killed one ranger and wounded four more. The group of rebels also threatened to kill all gorillas in the area. That summer the rangers found seven gorillas senselessly gunned down.

Much environmental damage is rooted in Congo's extreme poverty and history of conflict. To survive, villagers and refugees fleeing violence hunt wild animals to feed their families. They illegally grow crops or dig for minerals within park reserves. Lacking cooking gas or electricity, people cut trees and brush for fuel. This loss of woodlands, or deforestation, in turn leads to soil erosion. Without tree roots to hold it in place, the soil washes or blows away. Furthermore, many Congolese live without indoor plumbing or sewer systems. Filth washes into water sources, causing water pollution and spreading disease.

The difficulty of transporting timber long distances over poor roads has limited large-scale timber harvesting. Illegal logging, however, damages woodlands in the east, where loggers cut and sell timber to nearby countries. Environmentalists are concerned that logging destroys wildlife habitats. Since 2003 Congo's government has run tree-replanting programs to limit the damage.

Mining, logging, and industry bring Congo money, but they also damage the environment. To produce one diamond, for instance, workers must dig up and crush tons of rock. Fishing crews protest that Congo's oil fields in the Atlantic Ocean pollute ocean waters. Runoff from chemicals used in mining is another cause for concern. Workers pour cyanide, a toxic chemical, on piles of crushed rock to extract small amounts of gold. The poison drains into the surrounding earth and water.

Visit www.vgsbooks.com for links to websites with additional information about the Democratic Republic of Congo's land and resources. Check out the weather in Congo and learn about efforts to save mountain gorillas and other endangered animals.

Cities

Congo's government last took a census (official count) of the population in 1988, so experts must estimate current population figures for Congo's cities. About 30 percent of Congo's estimated 63 million citizens live in urban areas. The percentage grows as young villagers move to cities in search of jobs.

KINSHASA (population about 8 million) is the capital of Congo and the country's largest city. It sits on the Congo River, about 200 miles (320 km) inland from the Atlantic Ocean. The site was a small village in 1880, when Belgium's King Leopold II gave British explorer Henry M. Stanley a treaty to govern the area. The king made the village, then named Leopoldville, the capital of Congo Free State.

Downtown modern Kinshasa boasts skyscrapers, foreign-owned grocery stores, and wide streets. Well-off people live in the pleasant Gombe suburb, with modern services. The majority of Congo's non-African residents live there too. But most of the city's residents live in poverty in vast, sprawling suburbs. Residents grow food on every available bit of bare ground. In 2007 the government passed a five-year plan to spend $1.5 billion to renovate the city.

With one-third of Congo's industries and with good transportation links, Kinshasa is also the country's main economic center. The capital's factories produce textiles, clothing, footwear, and tires. Other industries include ship repair, sawmilling (timber processing), and palm oil processing. Kinshasa has a campus of the National University of Congo, as well as several other schools of higher education.

LUBUMBASHI (population about 1 million) was called Elizabethville during colonial times. The city sits on a high plain west of the Lualaba River, near the border of Zambia. Lubumbashi is the capital of Katanga, the heart of the nation's copper-mining industry.

Open-pit and underground mines dominate Lubumbashi. The city's factories process copper and refine the by-products of copper ore. Large piles of factory waste are visible from miles away, and factory

A haze of air pollution from industry covers the city of **Lubumbashi.** Residential neighborhoods like these sprawl out from the city's industrial heart.

chimneys spew thick smoke into the sky. Lubumbashi's other industrial products include cigarettes, textiles, shoes, and processed foods.

KISANGANI (population about 500,000) was formerly called Stanleyville. It is the capital of the Upper Congo area, which covers the northeastern part of the country. The city sits at the junction of the Congo and Tshopo rivers. However, 125 miles (200 km) of rapids and waterfalls separate the city from the navigable portion of the Congo. Railways and roads link the city to other parts of northeastern Congo. Kisangani also has a campus of the National University of Congo.

Once a fishing village and trading post, Kisangani became a major port for trade in farming and mining goods in the late 1800s. As in many other places, violence during Congo's civil wars rocked the city. Fighting killed many people and damaged houses, businesses, and the local economy.

KANANGA (population about 500,000) is the capital of West Kasai. Its name honors the leader of the local Lulua people. Situated on the Lulua River, the city is an administrative and transportation center. Kananga was also once the center of Congo's diamond industry. In 1970, however, it lost its position to Mbuji-Mayi, the capital of East Kasai. Since then, many of Kananga's roads and industries have declined.

HISTORY AND GOVERNMENT

The earliest-known inhabitants of Congo settled in the rain forest as long as ten thousand years ago. They established hunting and gathering communities. They are the ancestors of the Mbuti people who live in the present-day Congo Basin.

People who spoke Bantu languages began to move into Congo from western Africa after about 1000 B.C. *Bantu* means "people." The name refers to any group of African people whose members speak one of the Bantu languages. The Bantu in Congo were farmers and animal herders as well as hunters and gatherers. Over the course of many centuries, these peoples spread throughout the Congo Basin.

Many Bantu speakers settled south of Congo's rain forests in the grasslands. They made iron tools and fashioned copper into jewelry and into ingots (solid bars) used as money. Bantu groups spread the knowledge of metalworking throughout central Africa.

By A.D. 800, Congo contained a mixture of Bantu peoples. From about the twelfth century onward, several groups began to form kingdoms

led by nobles. West of Lake Tanganyika, archaeologists have found graves of these leaders. Their people had buried them with copper, iron, and ivory jewelry. Tombs in the Katanga region contain bracelets, bells, and other metal goods.

Kingdoms Arise

About 1400, ethnic groups from the north began to migrate into northern Congo. They intermarried with the Bantu peoples, and a new mosaic of cultures arose. At about the same time, the Bantu communities of western and southern Congo were combining into larger kingdoms.

The largest of the kingdoms were the Kongo, the Luba, the Lunda, and the Kuba. In each realm, the line of authority was strict. Local leaders, or chiefs, owed loyalty and goods to more powerful regional leaders. This system reached upward to the king.

Two other sizable Bantu kingdoms—the Teke and the Chokwe—also developed at this time. The Teke settled on both sides of the

Congo River in the northwest. The Chokwe lived near the upper Kwango and Kasai rivers in southwestern Congo.

◐ Kongo and Luba

The center of the Kongo kingdom lay north of the mouth of the Congo River. In the 1400s, this realm began to spread its power over parts of present-day Angola and the Republic of the Congo. The Kongo kingdom took conquered peoples into its population. Local leaders held religious as well as political power.

> When a Kongo king died, a group of nobility traditionally chose a new king from among his children. Eight men and four women of noble families held power in this royal council.

Like other Bantu people, Kongo's people practiced animism. This religious view is based on the belief that spirit, or conscious life, inhabits all things—living or not—including people, places, and natural events such as the weather.

In the mid-1400s, after the Kongo kingdom enlarged, villages in the southeastern grasslands began to combine into small states. Traditional stories say that an outside group of Bantu speakers, called the Lopwe, sped up the process by organizing the villages into a single political unit.

Under the skilled leadership of Lopwe kings, the Luba kingdom emerged. The Luba realm stretched between the Kasai River and Lake Tanganyika. Lopwe nobility dominated its strong government. Trade linked the Luba with merchants who lived near the Indian Ocean in eastern Africa.

◐ The Portuguese Arrive

While various kingdoms were forming in Congo, the European nation of Portugal was looking for ways to increase its power. Portuguese explorers arrived on Africa's coast looking for gold and grain. One of the first was Portuguese trader Diogo Cão. He reached the mouth of the Congo River in 1482. He soon made contact with the Kongo kingdom at its capital of Mbanzakongo (in present-day Angola).

The arrival of the Portuguese began a new era for Kongo and other kingdoms. Portugal wanted to control trade between Europe and Africa. The Portuguese brought European goods, technology, and religion. Roman Catholic missionaries came from Portugal to Kongo. These religious teachers wanted to convert the king and his family to the Catholic faith.

Nzinga Mbemba became Kongo's king in 1507. The king admired the ways of the Portuguese and tried to install European practices in his realm. He became a Catholic and took the name Afonso I. He signed trading contracts with Europeans and encouraged Christian missionary work. He ordered the destruction of items used in traditional religious worship. Afonso also allowed some of his subjects to be educated in Portugal.

Lunda

In the 1500s, the brother of the Luba king moved toward the southwest and founded the Lunda realm. It straddled the boundary of present-day Angola and Congo. After conquering the local leaders, the Lunda king let the former chiefs keep some power in exchange for money and goods. Lunda nobles took the status, name, and family of the conquered leaders.

The Slave Trade

Slavery had existed for centuries in some African cultures, including Kongo. Africans considered slaves to be full human beings. Slaves could hold important jobs and had some rights. When slaves gave birth, for instance, their owners could not sell the children.

The slave trade took on new aspects and greatly expanded after the European discovery of the Americas. Owners of plantations, or huge farms, in the New World began to look to Africa as a source of slave labor. Slave owners in the Americas considered the Africans racially inferior and without human rights.

Few Europeans went inland to capture slaves. The Portuguese preferred to deal with African brokers, who brought captives and goods to settlements near the coast. Portuguese merchants exchanged cloth, manufactured goods, and jewelry for ivory, copper, and slaves in the Kongo kingdom. They sent large numbers of enslaved Africans to labor on Portuguese plantations in Brazil, South America. Many slaves died in chains during the journey.

In this illustration, European ambassadors kneel in the court of Kongo's **King Afonso I** (center, seated).

A PLEA AGAINST THE SLAVE TRADE

In 1526 King Afonso I of Kongo sent a letter of protest (in Portuguese) to the king of Portugal. Afonso objected to the Portuguese carrying off thousands of his people into slavery. He wrote, "Each day the traders are kidnapping our people—children of this country... even people of our own family.... This corruption and depravity are so widespread that our land is entirely depopulated.... It is our wish that this kingdom not be a place for the trade or transport of slaves."

The king ignored Afonso's pleas, and the trade continued.

King Afonso originally agreed that slavers could take people captured in the area's frequent wars. Soon, however, the Portuguese were kidnapping villagers and even nobles. Afonso recognized that slave trading was rapidly reducing his country's population. He complained to the Portuguese king, who had no intention of ending the trade.

In the late 1500s, to maintain a constant supply of slaves, Portugal established Angola as a colony south of the Kongo kingdom. From this base, the Portuguese encouraged warlike African groups to raid the interior and kidnap people. Slave raids killed an average of one person for every one captured. Despite these practices, Portugal maintained peaceful ties with Kongo and continued to send missionaries to the kingdom.

Kongo Declines and Kuba Thrives

In 1568 a group of African warriors attacked the capital, Mbanzakongo, to take control of the slave trade. The Kongo king—Alvaro I—called for Portugal's help. Backed by Portuguese forces, Alvaro drove out the invaders in 1573. To repay Portugal for its aid, Alvaro allowed slave trading to increase and to reach farther inland.

Economic rivalry among European nations increasingly affected Congo's kingdoms. In the early 1600s, the seafaring Dutch were threatening Portugal's commercial power in Africa. In addition, Dutch, French, and British merchants arrived on the western African coast and began taking captives from Kongo.

The slave trade did not touch all communities in Congo at this time. The Mbuti lived deep in the Ituri rain forest, for instance, where outsiders never went. The Kuba had moved inland to the present-day Kasai region to escape Portuguese influence. The people of the twenty related Kuba groups fished and traded along the rivers.

Shamba Bolongongo, the son of a slave woman, became king of Kuba in the 1620s. He encouraged inventions in technology and architecture. He introduced corn, tobacco, and cassava (a starchy root) to Kuba farmers. The Portuguese had brought these crops from the Americas. Artists held a special place in this thriving society. Kuba weavers became famous for their decorated cloth and costumes. Sculptors created masks and treasures for the royal family.

Effects of the Slave Trade

Slave trading continued to weaken Kongo. War broke out between Portuguese-held Angola and Kongo in 1665. The Portuguese-backed Angolan soldiers easily defeated the weakened Kongo army. To further disrupt the kingdom, the Portuguese purchased prisoners of war as slaves.

After the decline of Kongo, the slave trade increased. Buyers from Europe and later the Americas took thousands of people from Congo every year. Slavery tore African families apart and caused political systems to break down. Local leaders rebelled against the more powerful central authorities. Many African authorities were making money from the trade.

By the 1700s, slave trading had grown so much that Europeans built special ports on the African coasts to handle the traffic. In time, other kingdoms in Congo took over the slave trade from Kongo. The Lunda realm expanded throughout the 1700s. It sent its warriors to raid Luba territories for slaves and ivory. They exchanged people with Europeans for goods and salt. The Lunda king also kept some of the captives to work on his farms.

In the 1800s, demand for slave labor was high in eastern Africa. Many Congolese people sold into slavery were sent eastward. Slaves were forced to march in chains, sometimes carrying elephants' ivory tusks long distances to ocean ports. Some brokers shipped their captives as far

Two **slave traders** *(in white)* drive chained captives through the jungle. Traders often killed captives who were sick or who refused to walk.

as the Middle East. By the mid-1800s, Swahili-speaking merchants from eastern Africa dominated the trade. While pursuing their interests, they often interfered with local Congolese politics. In time, Swahili became an important language in the Eastern Highlands.

One of the Swahili speakers was an Arab African trader named Tippu Tib. He reached Luba in the 1850s. With a staff of about four thousand people, he set up his own state on the Lualaba River. From there he traded slaves for many years. At about the same time, a merchant named Msiri acted as a go-between for Arab traders and Katanga leaders. Eventually, he established an operation similar to Tippu Tib's. It prospered from the sale of copper, ivory, and slaves.

Many European countries and the United States outlawed the slave trade (though not always slavery at home) in the early 1800s. However, illegal slave trading continued to flourish. Ultimately it devastated the populations of Africa's west coast.

Exploration and the Congo Free State

Looking for raw, natural materials to fuel Europe's expanding industries, Europeans explored Congo throughout the 1800s. In 1816 a British group sailed up the Congo River to Isangila Falls. They brought back detailed studies of the area. Other expeditions in the mid-1800s reached Lake Tanganyika.

Missionaries who wanted to spread their Christian religions also journeyed deep into Africa. The Scottish missionary David

This illustration from a British magazine from the early 1800s shows some Congolese clothing styles. Slaves carry the European shown in the back.

Explorer Henry Stanley founded this camp on the Congo River in the 1870s.

Livingstone increased knowledge of Congo through newspaper accounts of explorations he made from 1840 to 1872.

In 1874 a British American journalist named Henry M. Stanley sailed down the Congo River. He arrived at the Atlantic Ocean on March 12, 1877. His trip attracted the attention of King Leopold II of Belgium.

Leopold's ambition for territory and riches far exceeded the resources of his small European kingdom. In Stanley's reports, Leopold saw an opportunity to make money from the sale of Congo's rubber, ivory, and other natural resources. Leopold hired Stanley to explore the Congo Basin and to reach trade agreements with local leaders. In 1880 Stanley began his explorations, with African guides and porters to carry cargo and equipment. During the journey, he established the settlement of Leopoldville (modern Kinshasa).

Stanley returned to Europe with more than four hundred treaties he had persuaded Congolese leaders to sign. In these documents, Leopold claimed the rights to much of Congo's land, resources, and the labor of local people. The leaders hadn't understood how much they were giving away. In exchange, the Congolese were supposed to get improvements in living conditions and protection from slave trading. Instead, Leopold would institute a new kind of slavery.

In 1884 representatives of thirteen European nations met at the Berlin Conference to discuss dividing Africa into colonies. They did not include African leaders. The conference began the so-called Scramble for Africa, as European nations took control of almost all of Africa. In 1885 the conference recognized Congo as the personal property of Leopold II and called it the Congo Free State.

The word *free* in the Congo Free State refers to Leopold's plan that businesses from other countries could operate freely in his state. The king gave private European companies rights to collect rubber and ivory, to mine copper, and to grow crops on large tracts of land. In return, the companies paid the king part of their profits. Leopold also set up an administrative system to run his colony.

Centuries of slave raids had left central African kingdoms weak. Resistance to the Europeans was widespread, but it was not difficult for white men—armed with rifles—to take over control from local rulers. Europeans drew new borders with a lack of respect for ethnic groupings and traditions. The Belgians called all the people Congolese, though they belonged to more than two hundred different groups. Europeans did not settle in Congo in large numbers because of the uncomfortable climate.

The European companies passed laws that set the amounts of produce, such as rubber and food crops, that African locals had to grow for them. Mining companies marched men in chains to work hundreds of miles away. Despite the European ban on slavery, Africans worked for no pay and received little food. Officials often drove their workers mercilessly and punished or even killed people who resisted.

▶ Outcry

Leopold's extreme methods led to international disapproval. One of the first whistle-blowers was an African American journalist named George Washington Williams. He spent six months in Congo in 1890. Horrified, he wrote about the crimes he saw. For instance, he reported that authorities sometimes cut off

Heart of Darkness

In 1890 European writer Joseph Conrad worked on a riverboat in the Congo Free State. He had thought European civilization would help what he considered a savage land. Instead, the white men's greed and brutality horrified him. Conrad's experience became the basis of his famous short novel *Heart of Darkness*. In the book, he describes seeing slave laborers dying in the shade:

"Black shapes crouched, lay, sat between the trees leaning against the trunks, clinging to the earth . . . in all the attitudes of pain, abandonment, and despair. Another mine [explosive] on the cliff went off, followed by a slight shudder of the soil under my feet. The work was going on. The work! And this was the place some of the helpers had withdrawn to die.

"They were dying slowly—it was very clear. They were . . . nothing but black shadows of disease and starvation, lying confusedly in the greenish gloom."

King Leopold II ruled Belgium from 1865 until 1909. This portrait of the king dates to 1891.

workers' hands or feet if they did not obey.

Even in the face of a far greater force, Congo's people sometimes rose in revolt against their oppressors. In 1893 a local leader named Nzansu led rebels against a Belgian outpost that used slave labor. In response, armed forces working for the Belgians burned the rebels' villages, but Nzansu's rebellion continued for several months.

Missionaries and reporters continued to document Leopold's brutality against the Congolese. In the early 1900s, the reports caused an outcry in Europe and in the United States. People began to push their political leaders to change the situation. Historians consider this the first human rights movement of the twentieth century.

International criticism of Leopold's colonial rule became so great that on November 15, 1908, the Belgian parliament, or legislature, took over the region. The Congo Free State was made into a colony called the Belgian Congo. By then harsh conditions had killed as many as eight million Congolese.

The Belgian Congo

The Belgian parliament had authority over the Belgian Congo. But, in practice, a few powerful European companies ran the colony for Belgium. The companies controlled most of Congo's wealth. The Belgian nation—rather than the king or Congo—received the colony's profits.

Life for Congolese workers did not improve much. In 1910, for example, Belgian merchants organized a railway-building project. They needed trains to carry goods to port cities. Terrible working conditions during the railway's construction caused the death by accident, disease, and starvation of many Congolese. The abuses sparked labor riots, which colonial officials put down by force.

In the 1910s, Belgium was more concerned with events in Europe than with the Belgian Congo. The rivalry of Germany against France and Britain eventually led to the outbreak of World War I (1914–1918).

This 1917 French poster celebrated the bravery of **African soldiers in World War I.** Soldiers from the Belgian Congo fought against German forces stationed in Rwanda.

To strike at France, Germany occupied Belgium during the bloody war. The Belgian government fled to neighboring France.

Money from the Belgian Congo's exports helped to support the Belgian government in exile during the war. Congo also provided soldiers and raw materials to the countries allied against Germany. Congolese troops fought German forces in Germany's eastern African colonies and in Cameroon.

Between the World Wars

World War I ended with a German defeat in 1918. Afterward, Belgium turned its attention to its colonial activities. Like other European powers, Belgium saw itself as a caretaker for peoples the Belgians thought were not able to look after themselves. Africans disagreed with this view, but they had little power or opportunity to change it.

A class of Belgian civil servants (government workers) ran the colony. These professionals developed transportation and communications systems. Meanwhile, Belgium's economy continued to profit from the minerals and crops that Belgian-owned companies and plantations were producing in the colony.

Christian missionaries expanded their work in the Belgian Congo. Many of them believed that Congolese society would be improved if the people became Christians. Some Congolese accepted the Christian faith. Others resisted the missionaries' efforts at conversion. The colonial government supported mission schools. Teachers taught students job skills and the French language of the Belgian ruling class, as well as Christian beliefs.

By the 1920s, most Congolese workers mined copper, gathered rubber, and harvested crops for export. But diseases and harsh labor practices had greatly reduced the number of workers. Colonial officials started a public-health program to make sure that there would be enough healthy workers. In the mid-1920s, some companies improved working conditions and raised wages. The colony's economy faltered during the worldwide Great Depression (1929–1942).

The Road to Independence

War in Europe again affected the Belgian Congo when World War II (1939–1945) broke out. In 1940 Germany again invaded and occupied Belgium. Mines in Katanga supplied copper, tin, and other minerals to the nations fighting against Germany. Congolese soldiers fought German forces on the African continent in Libya and Ethiopia.

After Germany lost the war, money from the Belgian Congo's exports helped to rebuild Belgium. Yet the Congolese still had little influence on colonial government. In fact, strikes at several mining sites showed how deeply dissatisfied many Congolese were with colonial rule.

The Belgian Congo supplied uranium to the United States during World War II. The United States processed the radioactive mineral for use in the atomic bombs it dropped on Japan in August 1945, ending the war.

In the postwar era, colonized peoples around the world began to press for independence from foreign control. In Congo one such group was the Alliance of the Kongo People (ABAKO). ABAKO insisted that the colonial government provide freedom of the press and other civil rights that had been denied to the Congolese.

Belgian leaders did not grant these rights. But they responded to the pressure by declaring that they would slowly give up control of their colony over the next thirty years.

Unwilling to wait, the movement for national independence gained strength. Patrice Lumumba arose as an important leader of the National Congolese Movement (MNC). A charismatic leader, he stated that colonial rule was a kind of slavery in disguise and that it should end within two years.

In January 1959, the Belgian government's decision to cancel an ABAKO meeting sparked several days of rioting. Belgian troops killed dozens of people as they stamped out the riots.

This turmoil, as well as falling prices for minerals, persuaded Belgium that it could not hold onto its colony much longer. A meeting of leaders set June 30, 1960, as the date for independence. Far from taking thirty years, as Belgium had planned, Congo gained independence more quickly than almost any other colony in African history.

Independence and Lumumba

In preparation for independence, more than one hundred political parties ran in the May 1960 national elections. Patrice Lumumba, whom the Congolese saw as the hero of independence, became prime minister. Joseph Kasa-Vubu, the ABAKO leader and Lumumba's rival, became president. An elected parliament became the main lawmaking body.

The newly independent country did not enjoy the conditions necessary for success. Colonialism had weakened traditional African leadership. Belgian rulers had not educated the Congolese to run government and industry. With these unstable conditions, conflict flared between some Congolese and the tens of thousands of Belgians and other Europeans who remained in the country.

Lawlessness and revolt soon seized the country. Less than a week after independence, Congolese soldiers went on an unordered rampage, terrorizing and killing European residents. Europeans fled the country, leaving their possessions behind. Belgium sent in paratroopers to protect its citizens and business interests.

Not all Congolese leaders wanted Congo to be a united country. Moise Tshombe, the president of the copper-rich southern region of Katanga, wanted to control his own territory. On July 11, 1960, he declared Katanga independent from the Congo republic. The diamond-rich region of West Kasai followed.

Prime Minister Lumumba asked for peacekeeping troops from the United Nations (UN). Congo had recently joined this international organization for peace and development. The UN arrived to help restore order. It would not use UN troops to stop regions from seceding (splitting off), however. Lumumba therefore turned to the Soviet Union for help. This Communist country was an enemy of many Western nations (non-Communist nations west of Asia), including Belgium.

Supported by the Belgian government, President Kasa-Vubu decided to get rid of his rival, Lumumba. The army—led by Colonel

Patrice Lumumba, prime minister of Congo, speaks at a United Nations Security Council meeting in 1960.

Joseph-Désiré Mobutu—arrested the prime minister. In January 1961, Lumumba was taken to Katanga, where a firing squad executed him in the jungle.

Turmoil followed the murder of Lumumba. The regions of East Kasai and Kivu claimed their independence too, and the first Congo crisis continued. The UN, with strong backing from the United States, ended up using its troops to force Katanga and other regions to rejoin the Congo republic. With Western aid, the Congolese army also put down an uprising of Lumumba's supporters in 1963. The cost in lives and destruction was enormous.

▶ Mobutu Seizes Power

Regional rivalries among political parties made it nearly impossible for the national government to work. Soon it became deadlocked. In late 1965, Colonel Mobutu overthrew Kasa-Vubu in a nonviolent coup, or takeover.

Mobutu took control throughout the country. He ruled as a dictator, with absolute power. Tired of bloodletting, the Congolese accepted the dictator's rule with little resistance. Mobutu nationalized (switched from private to state ownership) copper production. He exiled his rivals and weakened his opposition by pitting ethnic groups against one another. Western nations supported Mobutu because he was anti-Communist. They didn't want the Soviet Union to gain control of African nations.

In the 1970 elections, Mobutu—the only candidate allowed to run—won a seven-year term as president. He got rid of the office of prime minister and made his party, the Popular Movement of the Revolution (MPR), the country's only legal political party.

President Mobutu raises a ceremonial staff as he returns from a 1977 diplomatic trip. The full version of his African name is Mobutu Sese Seko Kuku Ngbendu Wa Za Banga. The name is usually translated "The all-powerful warrior who, because of his endurance and inflexible will to win, will go from conquest to conquest leaving fire in his wake." Like a traditional African chief, Mobutu also wore a leopard skin cap.

In the 1970s, Mobutu began a program to strengthen the nation's pride in its African heritage. On October 27, 1971, for example, he changed the Congo's name to the Republic of Zaire. The name is from the Bantu word *nzari*, meaning "river." The government also replaced the European names of most of Zaire's cities and regions with African names. In another step toward Africanization, Mobutu insisted that citizens adopt African names and stop wearing Western clothing. He changed his name from Joseph-Désiré Mobutu to Mobutu Sese Seko.

◉ Hard Times in Zaire

Zaire struggled economically in the mid-1970s. Poor management drove industries and farms into ruin. Congo's political involvement in a civil war in Angola also weakened the country. The conflict closed Angola's Benguela Railroad. This was Zaire's main route for sending copper to the Atlantic coast. Mobutu supported the losing side in the Angolan civil war.

Zaire's problems continued in the 1980s. The annual rate of inflation (rising prices) reached 100 percent. To reduce it, the government cut imports, health services, school programs, and social welfare benefits. These measures hurt most Zaireans, except the wealthy. But they did not curb the inflation rate.

In 1984 Mobutu won a third term as president in a rigged election. He pledged to improve transportation, education, and health services. In reality, the standard of living continued to decline. The gap between rich and poor continued to widen.

In the late 1980s, international banks and Western governments accused Mobutu and his followers of corrupt practices. Lenders could not trace much of the money loaned to Zaire. Many believed the funds had ended up in Mobutu's personal treasury, which was estimated to be worth $5 billion. Some lenders, including Belgium and the United States, withheld more aid until stronger democratic practices were in place.

Observers called Mobutu's government a kleptocracy, which means "rule by thieves." A minority of Congolese grew rich through corrupt practices. They flaunted their wealth with expensive status symbols. For instance, Zaire had more Mercedes-Benz sedans (elite German cars) per person than any other African nation.

In 1990, under political pressure, Mobutu promised to move his country toward a freer political system. But he broke his promise. The country's stability wavered. In 1991 unpaid soldiers looted stores and destroyed property. Riots erupted, and chaos reigned. European professionals fled, leaving the schools and clinics they ran throughout the country understaffed. The collapsed economy led to food shortages and a decline in medical supplies.

In 1992 health-care professionals counted more than eleven thousand cases of the deadly disease AIDS in Congo. Without adequate health care and education, the illness spread quickly.

Congo's unstable situation worsened in 1994. That year members of the Hutu ethnic group in Rwanda mass murdered Rwanda's ethnic Tutsi population. The Tutsi army then defeated the Hutu government of Rwanda. In the aftermath, more than one million Hutus fled to eastern Zaire, where both ethnic groups also live. Soon the Hutu refugees and some of Zaire's military began killing Zaireans of Tutsi ancestry.

The First Congo War

Mobutu continued to refuse to hold elections and to share power. In August 1996, he went to Switzerland for cancer treatments. While Mobutu was abroad, armed Tutsi citizens of Zaire captured much of eastern Congo. Members of other ethnic groups joined the rebels too. Troops from Rwanda, Uganda, and Burundi invaded Zaire and aided the rebels. Longtime Mobutu opponent Laurent-Désiré Kabila led the rebellion, which later was called the First Congo War (1996–1997). It soon grew into a national revolt to throw Mobutu out of office.

In December 1996, Mobutu returned to Zaire. The anti-Mobutu rebels marched through the country. They massacred Hutu men,

Young men in Kinshasa smash government guns in May 1997. They are celebrating Laurent Kabila's overthrow of Mobutu's government that year.

women, and children. Government army troops, for their part, also looted, raped, and killed civilians. In response, many untrained young Congolese men and boys joined Kabila's rebels.

In April 1997, Mobutu fled the country. Kabila's troops entered Kinshasa, and Kabila declared himself president. He renamed the country the Democratic Republic of Congo.

At first, the people of Congo were glad to be rid of Mobutu, who died in exile in September. But Kabila did little to improve their quality of life. While he promised democracy, he outlawed other political parties and made laws to give himself near-absolute power. His loyal but undisciplined teen soldiers, armed with assault rifles, patrolled Kinshasa and the nation's roads.

The Second Congo War

Kabila's government was soon competing with various rebel groups for control of Congo's land and resources. The struggle grew worse as members of more foreign armies became involved. In August 1998, rebels backed by Rwanda and Uganda rose up against Kabila in Congo. Zimbabwe, Angola, and Namibia sent troops to side with Kabila. The anti-Kabila rebels took control of much of eastern Congo in August. Once again, civil war raged in Congo.

During the Second Congo War (1998–2003), civilians endured horror at the hands of warring groups. Rebels forced children to be soldiers. Armed groups contributed to the spread of AIDS by rape and sexual slavery.

All sides used their soldiers to make money. Zimbabwe's troops took over Congolese copper mines. Rwanda and Uganda plundered diamonds and gold. Meanwhile, Congo's standard of living fell disastrously low. More people died of starvation and sickness during the war than from outright violence.

In January 2001, an assassin shot President Kabila to death. His son Joseph Kabila took over the presidency. The civil war raged on.

Meanwhile, in an effort to clear past wrongs, in 2002 the Belgian government apologized to the Congolese people for its role in the 1961 murder of Prime Minister Lumumba. The Belgians admitted that their government had worked to get rid of the elected leader, though they did not actually order his death.

Hopes for peace grew in 2002. UN-sponsored peace talks between Congo's warring parties began in South Africa. By the end of the year, the government and the main rebel groups had signed a deal to end fighting.

Eight other African countries and thousands of UN peacekeeping troops from other countries were involved in the Second Congo War (1998–2003). The conflict is sometimes called Africa's First World War.

Under the terms of the agreement, President Kabila led a transitional government. Set up in 2003, it would govern until elections could be held. Four vice presidents from opposition and rebel groups served alongside the president.

A Fragile Peace

A United Nations peacekeeping force oversaw Congo's transition to peace, which held in most of the country. In the east, however, fighting continued off and on between government forces and rebels. By this time, about one million Congolese in the east had lost their homes due to the war. They became refugees in their own country. In 2005 rebels in the northeast murdered nine UN peacekeepers from Bangladesh. The peacekeeping offensive in return killed more than fifty rebels.

Troubles in neighboring countries also spilled over into Congo. Rebels from Uganda's violent Lord's Resistance Army (LRA), for instance, entered Congo, increasing tension between Congo and Uganda, which had sent troops into Congo during the Second Congo War. Despite the strains, Congo's government held together. Legislators from different parties worked together to write a new constitution. In late 2005, voters approved the constitution, which became law in February 2006.

Elections for Congo's president and legislature occurred in July 2006. With no clear winner in the presidential race, a runoff election between Joseph Kabila and Jean-Pierre Bemba was held on October 29. Violence erupted between supporters of the two candidates. Kabila

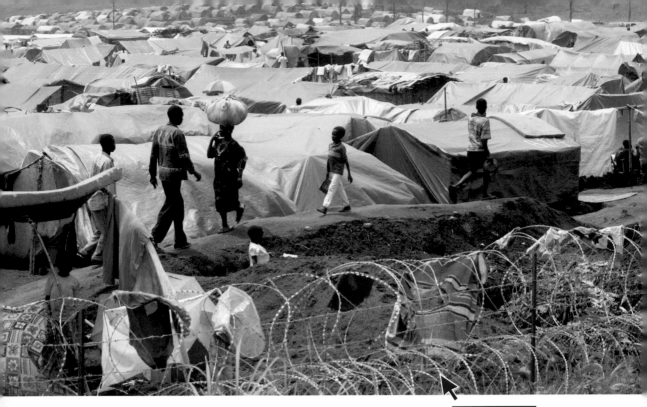

Families fleeing fighting in the Ituri region take shelter in a refugee camp near Bunia. The camps lack sanitary facilities and clean water.

won the runoff election. He officially became president in December. Bemba fled the country.

Peace remains fragile in Congo. President Kabila's government does not control large parts of eastern Congo. The more than sixteen-thousand-troop UN peacekeeping force in Congo is the largest in the world. The peacekeepers have disarmed thousands of former militia members. They are mostly stationed in the east, where rebels continue to rob, rape, and murder. Meanwhile, most Congolese throughout the country struggle to survive poverty, disease, and hunger.

Joseph Kabila

◉ Government

Congo adopted a new constitution in 2005. Laws require all Congolese citizens eighteen years and older to vote.

Citizens elect the president to a five-year term, with a limit of two terms. The president is head of the executive branch. The president chooses cabinet members to help run the government. The cabinet of advisers is called the National Executive Council.

The bicameral (two-house) legislature is composed of the National Assembly and the Senate. Voters elect the 500 assembly members to five-year terms. Local assemblies elect the 120 senators to five-year terms.

Congo's judges hear cases at the local and appeals levels. The Supreme Court is the judicial branch's highest court. It can judge cases from all other courts.

For the purposes of local administration, Congo is divided into ten regions. The capital city of Kinshasa forms a separate, eleventh region. The 2005 constitution further subdivides the regions into twenty-six provinces. The government appoints governors and vice-governors to run each province. Chiefs maintain order in the smallest administrative units, known as collectives.

The United Nations and Congo's national army have collected and destroyed thousands of weapons from former rebels in northeastern Congo. A local group of women, the Ituri's Mothers' Forum, approved of the action. One of the women said, "We, the mothers, have been very disturbed by these arms. We could not go to the market or to fields. Many people have been injured because of these arms."

—quoted in a United Nations report at http://www.irinnews.org/ report.aspx?ReportId=72289

Visit www.vgsbooks.com for links to websites with additional information about political developments in the Democratic Republic of Congo. Link to the latest news headlines, and follow efforts to control militia violence in the country's eastern regions.

THE PEOPLE

Congo last held an official census of its population in 1988. At that count, the population was 34.7 million people. Experts estimate that Congo's population has reached 63 million. Almost half of the nation's citizens are younger than 15 years old. With the large number of young women coming into childbearing years, the population will continue to grow rapidly. The average Congolese woman gives birth six or seven times in her life. Congo's population is expected to reach 108 million by 2025. Congo's government views the birthrate as satisfactory.

Congo's population density is 69 people per square mile (27 people per sq. km). The average for Africa south of the Sahara (the desert that covers much of northern Africa) is 82 people per square mile (32 per sq. km)—a figure that is about the same as in the United States. Farming employs two-thirds of Congo's people. Most of Congo's people are poor, and 70 percent live in rural areas. Most Congolese have a hard time making enough money to feed, clothe, and shelter their families.

The United Nations offers the Human Development Index (HDI) as one way to look at a nation's people. Key indicators such as life expectancy, literacy, and average income determine the HDI. The United States ranks 8 out of 177 countries. Former powers in Congo, Portugal ranks 28 and Belgium ranks 13. Congo ranks 167—one of the least developed countries in the world.

Ethnic Groups

More than two hundred ethnic groups live in Congo, giving the nation a rich variety of cultures and languages. Most groups live, work, and socialize together in harmony. Intermarriage among groups is common. People usually settle tensions among themselves peaceably. The nation's ethnic violence has occurred when political enemies have used ethnic differences for their own purposes.

No one of the Congo's groups makes up over 10 percent of the total population. Most Congolese fall into one of four major categories.

About 70 percent of the population belong to Bantu-speaking groups. Another 20 percent are of Sudanic background, meaning their ancestors came from lands north of Congo, probably from southern Sudan. The Mbuti and other rain-forest dwellers form almost 7 percent of the population. Members of Nilotic groups—people with historic ties to regions near the Nile River—make up 3 percent. About fifty thousand Westerners, mostly Belgians, also make their homes in Congo. Small numbers of people from western Africa, Lebanon, and India make up an important merchant class in Congo.

Among the largest Bantu-speaking groups are the Mongo, the Luba, the Lunda, the Kongo, and the Lulua. The Mongo live throughout the cuvette and in a large area of the Southern Uplands bordered by the Lulonga, Momboyo, and Lualaba rivers. The Luba, who dwell in Kasai and Katanga, tend to be highly independent of the central government. Many Luba are mission educated and hold positions of authority in business and in the civil service of Katanga. The Lunda, a people ethnically related to the Luba, dominate southern Katanga, southwestern Kasai, and the southeastern tip of the Bandundu region.

The Zande and Mangbetu are Sudanic peoples. They live near the Ubangi and Uele rivers.

The Mbuti speak Efe, a Sudanic language. Their lifestyles have changed little since ancient times. They still hunt and gather food in

People from many ethnic and religious backgrounds fill a busy street in the town of Goma. Popular fashions include both Western and local clothing.

Mbuti women prepare a meal in the Ituri Forest. The Mbuti make their homes by fastening tree bark to a framework of flexible branches.

the rain forests of Congo. The Mbuti number less than 100,000 and are scattered in regions near the equator.

Nilotic peoples, such as the Alur and the Kakwa, make their homes in the northeastern part of the country. Nilotic groups also live in Uganda, Rwanda, and Burundi.

The Mbuti call themselves *Ba miki ba ndula*, which means "children of the forest." They are some of the smallest people in the world. Adults average about 4 feet 7 inches (1.4 m) high. Their small size allows them to move easily through their dense forest environment.

Ways of Life

Bantu culture gives most Congolese a shared social outlook. The general attitude is one of concern for the well-being of other people. Congolese of all groups have strong family ties. Most families are large and often include grandparents and other family members.

Villages are the most common unit of social organization in Congo. Residents are often related to one another. People build their houses from sun-dried mud bricks or branches covered with dried mud. They roof them with grass thatch.

Villagers usually are able to grow and gather only enough food to feed their families. Men hunt and fish. Women cultivate crops, collect firewood and water, and cook. Farmwork involves hours of backbreaking work with handheld tools. Women also care for the children and the

A **young woman from Goma** shows off her hairstyle, which is popular in eastern Congo.

house. They sell produce and goods at local open-air markets. Because of this work, they are often the main moneymakers in a family.

Children take on responsibility at an early age. Older children commonly share the jobs of pounding cassava or dried bananas into flour and watching the younger children while their parents work. Children are taught to be polite and to obey adults.

Marriage in Congo involves the whole family, not just the dating couple. Parents traditionally help to arrange their children's marriages. Polygyny, or the practice of a husband having more than one wife at a time, is common.

Like other developing countries in Africa, Congo has a very small middle class—based largely in cities. The nation's economy is weak, and wages are low. Therefore, most salaried workers, urban professionals, and businesspeople need second jobs to support their families.

The rapid growth of the nation's cities has created a large number of urban poor people. Most have arrived from rural areas in search of jobs and schooling, which are hard to get. Without work, they end up living in slums lacking sanitary and social services.

Most Congolese in urban areas wear Western clothing. In rural areas, some Congolese wear traditional clothing, sometimes mixed with Western styles. Women often wear a long, sewn dress made of 5 yards (5 m) of printed fabric. The dress is called a *liputa* in the Lingala language. Women may also wrap their heads in colorful cloth. Different groups wear different styles. Men and women Mbuti who live in the rain forest, for instance, traditionally wear loincloths made of bark cloth. Mbuti men make the cloth by stripping trees and beating the inner bark until soft. The women dye and decorate the cloth.

Education

Congo has historically suffered from a lack of well-funded schools. Since the civil war ended in 2003, the government has spent millions of dollars to fund basic education. Congolese laws require children to attend school for six years, beginning when they are six years old. Secondary education is not compulsory, or required by law. Students begin secondary school at twelve years old and continue for up to six years. The nation still lacks enough schools, teachers, and supplies to meet its citizens' needs. Only 33 percent of Congo's children go to primary school, and 12 percent attend secondary school. About 65 percent of Congolese are literate, or able to read and write basic sentences. The unequal literacy rate for males (76 percent) and females (55 percent) reflects the fact that more boys than girls go to school. Families often view boys as more worth educating and keep girls home to help with work.

One of the government's main goals at high school and college levels is to train Congolese in key technical and managerial skills needed to run their country. Most of the nation's university graduates receive their degrees from one of the campuses of the National University of Congo, which are at Kinshasa, Kisangani, Kananga, and Lubumbashi.

CHILD SOLDIERS

One of the worst legacies of Congo's civil war is the use of child soldiers. Rebel groups took thousands of children from their villages and forced them to choose between joining the militia or death. The militia members trained the children to be fighters or servants. One-third of the children were girls as young as ten. Many ended up as so-called soldiers' wives, or sex slaves.

Returning young soldiers to civilian life is one of the biggest challenges facing the country. Congo is making a major effort to disarm soldiers of all ages, especially the young ones. Shame and fear of burdening their families keep many young people from returning home. Unable to read or write, some expect they will never get jobs, if jobs even exist. Many young people who are at least eighteen join the Congolese army instead. Some even choose to return to rebel life.

Despite the presence of UN peacekeepers in areas where rebels still operate, armed groups continue to recruit children. In some cases, a life with the rebels appeals to children with little food, education, or hope. Rebel armies offer food, power, and some status to young soldiers.

◉ Health

Congo's medical facilities are severely limited. Medicines and medical equipment are in short supply. Only 1 doctor exists for every 1,000 people. Only 45 percent of Congo's population has access to clean water, and 80 percent lack sanitary facilities, such as sewers. Diseases such as hepatitis A and typhoid fever spread quickly in such conditions. Furthermore, widespread malnutrition contributes to people's inability to fight off disease.

In Congo, life expectancy at birth averages 50 years (49 years for men and 52 for women). This is very low compared to industrialized countries such as Belgium, where life expectancy averages 79 years. But it is about average for African nations south of the Sahara, which suffer some of the worst health statistics in the world.

Congo's infant mortality rate—95 deaths per 1,000 live births—is 5 more deaths than the average for sub-Saharan Africa. In comparison, Portugal averages 3.8 deaths per 1,000 babies. One of the leading causes of death among Congolese infants and young children is severe malnutrition, a result of the nation's protein-poor diet. Few Congolese children receive shots against common diseases such as measles. For every 1,000 children, 205 will not live to their fifth birthday.

Malaria is common throughout Congo. Mosquito bites spread the parasites that infect human blood with this disease. Malaria racks the

Children stand beside their home in a Kinshasa slum. Heavy rains flooded the area and brought disease-carrying sewage into streets and homes.

body with fevers and chills and can cause death. It is a leading killer of children. The tsetse fly spreads trypanosomiasis (sleeping sickness) to humans and animals in low-lying areas. The disease makes humans too weak and tired to work. Infected cattle slowly waste away. Outbreaks of cholera, yellow fever, the Ebola virus, and hemorrhagic fever also occur. Dysentery (severe diarrhea) and many kinds of parasites are also major hazards to public health.

HIV/AIDS (human immunodeficiency virus/acquired immunodeficiency syndrome) threatens all Congolese. Spread by body fluids, the disease has infected 3.2 percent of the adult population. While this is lower than sub-Saharan Africa's average of 6.1 percent, it means that more than 1.1 million Congolese suffer from this disease, which destroys their immune systems. High death rates among adults leave thousands of Congolese children orphans.

Congolese seek modern medical treatment, when available, for illnesses. People also depend on traditional cures from village healers. These specialists treat wounds and illnesses with medicines made from plants. They also perform surgical procedures. Members of international health organizations recognize the healers' effectiveness in certain areas. They are especially helpful in curing malaria, dysentery, infections, and diseases carried by parasites.

Visit www.vgsbooks.com for links to websites with additional information about life in the Democratic Republic of Congo. Find health statistics and learn about international aid organizations seeking to help create better conditions for Congo's people.

CULTURAL LIFE

The art of Congo's past kingdoms is famous throughout the world. Art museums and collectors worldwide highly value traditional items made for royal or sacred rituals as well as for daily use. In many of Congo's kingdoms, skilled wood-carvers created splendid masks, drums, thrones, and other art objects. Complex geometric patterns decorate the sculpted pieces. Craftspeople used natural materials such as raffia (a strawlike fiber) to produce baskets, mats, and textiles with intricate patterns. Artists richly adorned clothing with embroidery and beads.

The arrival of European missionaries, slave traders, and colonial rulers greatly influenced Congo culture. Europeans generally had little or no respect for African traditions. Missionaries and business owners broke up traditional ways of life. Africans sent as slaves to the Americas, however, carried with them their beliefs and arts that would eventually make their way into general American culture.

The arts of Congo attracted the interest of a group of artists in Paris in the early 1900s. The visual and emotional power of African art helped

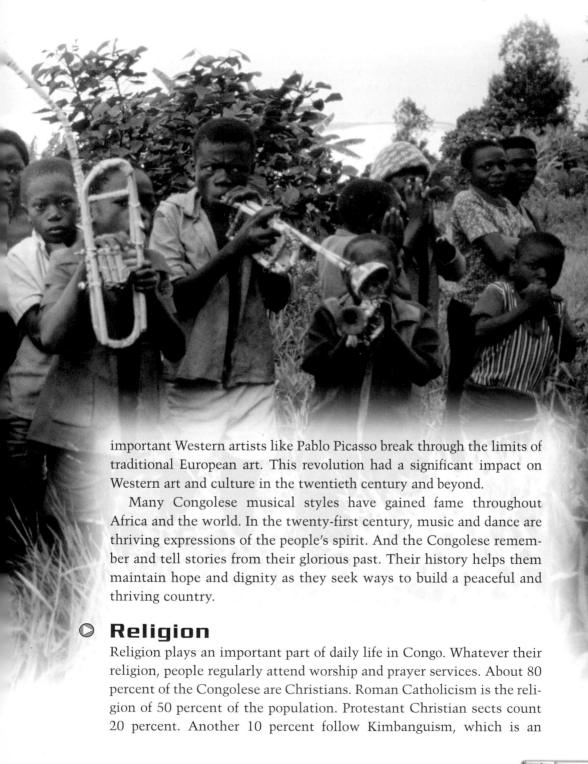

important Western artists like Pablo Picasso break through the limits of traditional European art. This revolution had a significant impact on Western art and culture in the twentieth century and beyond.

Many Congolese musical styles have gained fame throughout Africa and the world. In the twenty-first century, music and dance are thriving expressions of the people's spirit. And the Congolese remember and tell stories from their glorious past. Their history helps them maintain hope and dignity as they seek ways to build a peaceful and thriving country.

Religion

Religion plays an important part of daily life in Congo. Whatever their religion, people regularly attend worship and prayer services. About 80 percent of the Congolese are Christians. Roman Catholicism is the religion of 50 percent of the population. Protestant Christian sects count 20 percent. Another 10 percent follow Kimbanguism, which is an

As conditions in Congo worsened during the Second Congo War, some people turned to new religious sects, especially in Kinshasa. More than four hundred sects flourish in the capital city of 8 million people. Many model themselves on born-again Christian evangelical groups. But some are violent. The forty-member Army of Heaven, for instance, terrorized Kinshasa briefly in 2004.

indigenous (native) form of Christianity. Its founder, Simon Kimbangu, started the sect in the 1920s. It officially calls itself the Church of Jesus Christ of Earth by the Prophet Simon Kimbangu. Kimbanguism strictly follows the Bible. It promotes African culture but rejects traditional rituals. This church was the first independent African church admitted to the World Council of Churches. The council encourages cooperation and good will among all Christian sects.

Age-old African belief systems remain the religion of 10 percent of Congolese. These traditional faiths vary widely. Generally they are based on animism—the belief that everything, living or not, is interconnected and alive with spiritual power. People who practice traditional religions believe that certain people can communicate with the spirit world. Some of their rituals attempt to influence the forces that govern natural cycles, such as rainfall or fertility. Other rites honor ancestors or celebrate the passage from one stage of life to another. In some ceremonies, people dance all day and night until they feel the presence of spirits of animals or ancestors. Many Congolese combine some elements of Christian and traditional African beliefs.

The remaining 10 percent of Congolese are Muslims and follow the Islamic faith. They are the descendants of Arab and African traders who came to Congo from eastern Africa.

Music and Dance

Music and dance have always enjoyed an important place in Congo. In the southern savannas, orchestras of the Mangbetu ethnic group use wooden gongs, rectangular drums, large iron bells, and ivory horns with leather handles. The beating of drums and the clinking of metal bracelets accompany the dances of the Ngbandi group.

The Mongo people perform a ballet called the *bobongo*, in which several groups are onstage at once. The accompanying instruments include the *bonkwasa*, a percussion instrument made of bamboo stems. Musicians also play the *longombe*, a large, five-stringed harp mounted on a box.

Intore dancers perform a warrior dance at Lake Kivu. Men and women of the Intori have different traditional dances.

Lunda dancers perform to the music of the *njimba*. This curved xylophone is made with thin wooden slats set on gourds of different sizes. Congo's Intore dancers enjoyed a favored role at the royal courts of the 1400s and 1500s. The Intore still perform in the cities of Rutshuru and Boma.

Since independence in 1960, jazz bands have had a strong impact on the nation's musical tastes. Congo jazz and *soukous*—from a Lingala word meaning "shake," also called the African rumba—led the early jazz scene. Soukous's rhythms are lively, upbeat, and very danceable. Villages as well as cities boast clubs where fans can hear hit tunes. Musician Luambo Makiadi, known as Franco, led the O.K. Jazz Band in the 1960s and 1970s. Its fame spread throughout Africa. Franco's rivals include Kabasele and his African Jazz Band and Tabu Ley Rochereau.

Tabu Ley gained an international following by fusing elements of Congolese folk music with American soul and Caribbean and Latin rhythms. In the 1980s, he promoted the career of Mbilia Bel. She rose to fame and became known as the queen of Congolese rumba. In 2005 the government appointed Tabu Ley to be vice-governor of the city of Kinshasa.

Antoine Koffi Olomide rose to worldwide fame in the 1990s. In his deep, smooth voice, he sings a slow style of soukous, which he calls tcha tcho. Olomide also performs fast, hip-swaying dance music called *soukous ndombolo*. He tours widely with his band and released his twenty-eighth album in 2005. Bands from Congo that have won worldwide fame include Zaiko Langa Langa and Wenge Musica.

The Visual Arts

Congo has a rich artistic heritage. Craftspeople from many regions of the country carved masks and statues of wood or stone. Regarded as

Kuba mask

sources of spiritual power, masks appear in many ceremonies. Their keepers usually hide the masks when not in use.

Scholars of art consider Kuba masks among the finest in Congo. Kuba masks depict famous leaders of the Kuba kingdom. The Chokwe people create masks and intricate thrones, some in the shape of human figures. The Yaka people of the Bandundu region are famous for masks worn in dance. The Yaka also produce jewelry and canes carved in the likenesses of their ancestors.

Folk art is part of daily life around the country. Artisans create beautiful jewelry, baskets, and wood items for use. The Mangbetu people in southern Congo decorate and paint their dwellings in elaborate styles.

Modern artists depict their own lively, individual visions. Bodys Isek Kingelez (b. 1948) began his career restoring traditional masks in the National Museum of Kinshasa. In his own sculptures, he cuts, colors, and glues together found objects—such as bottle caps, tinfoil, and cardboard—to create fantastic, detailed scenes. His sculpture *Ville Fantôme* (Phantom City) combines the actual architecture of Kinshasa with the artist's imaginative buildings.

Chéri Samba (b. 1956) is a founder of the Popular Painting Movement, based in Kinshasa. As a child, he sold his humorous drawings outside his

Chéri Samba's painting *Little Kadogo* depicts a child soldier.

school. His paintings sometimes include words and often comment on Congo's pleasures and problems. His painting *Little Kadogo*, for instance, depicts a boy soldier surrounded by tropical flowers. In 2007 the famous Tate Modern museum in London, England, included Samba's art in its first-ever show of contemporary African art.

Self-trained painter Monsengwo Kejwamfi (1950–2001), known as Moke, was another founder of the movement. With humor and compassion, the painter portrayed Kinshasa's street life and all-night parties.

⊙ Language

Congo's different ethnic groups speak many different languages. The country's main communications take place in one of the four official Bantu languages—Lingala, Swahili (also called Kiswahili), Kikongo, or Tshiluba. Lingala contains many French words. It is the major language of people along the Congo River from Kinshasa to Kisangani. Members of the Congolese armed forces and government workers commonly speak it. Swahili contains many Arabic words. It dominates the Eastern Highlands. People living in the west between Kinshasa and the Atlantic Ocean—the region of the ancient Kongo kingdom—speak Kikongo. People in both of the Kasai regions and in some parts of Katanga speak Tshiluba, the Luba language. Most Congolese know one or more of several Bantu languages, which can be mutually understood by most Bantu-speaking people.

About 10 percent of Congolese speak French, the nation's fifth official language. Belgian colonial officials brought French to the region. Urban people might speak a mix of French and their native language.

⊙ Literature

Traditionally, Bantu speakers memorized their history and passed it on through the spoken word. Generations of storytellers preserved oral literature—including folktales and poems. Since colonial times, efforts have been made to write down the stories and legends of Congo's many groups. During the colonial period, the French-language poet Antoine-Roger

SOME THINGS SURVIVE

In the region where the Congo River enters the Atlantic Ocean, people have spoken the Kikongo language for generations. Slave traders took many people from this region to sell in the United States. While slave owners tried to strip slaves of their culture, traces of Kikongo survive in the modern United States. Language scholars have found that parts of the language exist in the Gullah dialect, spoken in the islands off the coast of South Carolina and Georgia.

Bolamba drew upon such ancient tales for his work *Esanzo, Songs of My Country*.

Independence in 1960 inspired a rush of Congolese creativity. Many authors expressed themselves in political writings and historical accounts. Playwrights made some of the most notable contributions. In the 1970s, Lisembe Elébé produced plays about striking workers, village life, and the religious leader Simon Kimbangu.

Modern Congo has a very small publishing industry, producing fewer than one hundred books a year. Most Congolese authors write in French. Dieudonné Mutombo, Mbwil a Mpang Ngal, and Vumbi Yoka Mudimbe are among the best-known postindependence novelists. These writers choose topics that range from the history of independence to the demands of a rapidly changing society.

Amba Bongo is a Congolese writer who lives in London because of Congo's lack of political freedom. She writes her novels in French. Her second novel, *Cécilia*, portrays a young woman living with AIDS who decides to stop keeping her disease a secret. Bongo believes the story is a common one for many men and women in Africa and around the world.

Frederick Kambemba Yamusangie is a Congolese novelist, playwright, and poet. Like Bongo, he lives in Great Britain, but he writes in English about Congo. His novel *Full Circle* (2003) concerns a boy moving to a new village.

> Visit www.vgsbooks.com for links to websites with additional information about art, literature, and music from the Democratic Republic of Congo. Read excerpts from Congolese literature and play samples of Congo's traditional and contemporary music.

Media

Reporters in Congo have long worked in a climate of violent unrest and political uncertainty. Reporters Without Borders, an international group for free speech, reports that media workers in Congo face arrest, threats, and violence. Reporters exposing corruption are at the most risk. Despite restrictions, journalists sometimes do criticize the government. Some publications express the views of opposition parties.

Congo has several daily newspapers. Dozens of private TV stations and more than one hundred private radio stations broadcast music and news. The state controls the largest broadcasting network. The state-controlled radio station Voice of Congo broadcasts in French, Swahili, Lingala, Tshiluba, and Kikongo.

Residents of Kinshasa follow the 2006 national runoff election on front pages displayed on the street. Readers can buy national and local newspapers in French, Swahili, and several other languages.

The United Nations helped launch Radio Okapi in 2002. The mostly Congolese broadcasters provide news, music, and information about UN activities. This politically independent network works to increase communication among different groups.

Sports, Socializing, and Holidays

Soccer, called football in Congo, is the nation's most popular sport. Other organized sports are rare in Congo. Most citizens and the government do not have money for sports equipment and training.

The Congolese enjoy socializing and visiting. Both rural and urban people enjoy gatherings that include dancing and music. Visiting friends and family is important to the Congolese. Most visiting takes place in people's houses. The host usually offers refreshments of some kind.

National holidays in Congo are New Year's Day, Commemoration of the Martyrs of Independence (honoring people who struggled for independence, January 4), Labor Day (May 1), Independence Day (June 30), Parents' Day (August 1), and Veterans' Day (November 17). Easter falls in March or April and Christmas on December 25. Muslims celebrate Islamic holidays. They do not eat or drink anything from sunrise to sunset during the holy month of Ramadan. Villagers also celebrate harvest festivals and other important events with music and dance.

Food

The Congolese eat a light breakfast—perhaps yesterday's leftovers or bread with tea. The main meal of the day is eaten in the late afternoon or early evening. Congolese generally grow their own food or purchase it daily from open-air markets. Most people cannot usually afford meat. They rely on starchy foods, such as cassava (manioc, or tapioca), rice, potatoes, yams, beans, and sorghum (a grain). Food is sometimes hard to find, and malnutrition and starvation threaten many Congolese.

Fufu is a sticky, breadlike dish made with cassava flour. It is a common staple food in Congo, like wheat bread elsewhere. Cassava is also the base of a dish called *chikwangue*. To prepare the dish, cooks make a paste of pounded cassava roots. They thicken the paste, wrap it in banana leaves, and boil it. Congolese cooks season food with palm oil, tiny hot peppers, and fresh ginger.

The many varieties of bananas, including plantains, provide a staple food rich in nutrients. Cooks steam, boil, or dry bananas. Ground dried bananas provide flour. Other common fruits include mangoes, oranges, papaya, and coconuts. Vegetables such as greens, corn, and sweet potatoes often appear in ordinary meals.

On special occasions, people might dine on *moambe* (stew). Chicken moambe is cooked in palm oil with peanut sauce, spinach, spices, and rice. *Makobe*, fish prepared in leaves, is another favorite main course. People also like to eat honey and honeycomb as a treat. Rural people earn money by selling honey they collect.

Insects eaten as snacks are an excellent source of protein. Favorites include termites, caterpillars, grasshoppers, and palm grubs (the larvae of rhinoceros beetles), dug out of palm trees.

Street vendors and restaurants offer soft drinks, fruit juices, and sparkling waters. For adults, popular drinks include the nation's many types of beer. Palm wine made from the sap of palm trees is common too.

A Libinza woman prepares to cook a meal of grubs collected from tree bark.

SPINACH WITH PEANUT SAUCE

This dish is common throughout central Africa. Spinach and peanuts are native to Africa, and the Portuguese introduced green peppers and tomatoes from South America. Cooks also prepare other greens, such as cassava leaves or collards, this way.

1 onion, finely chopped

I green bell pepper, seeded and chopped

2 tablespoons vegetable oil

1 tomato, chopped

¼ teaspoon salt

dash of black pepper

dash of cayenne (red) pepper

I pound fresh spinach, washed, stems removed, or 1 pound frozen spinach

¼ cup of water

½ cup peanut butter*

1. On medium heat, fry the onion and green pepper in oil in large frying pan for 10 minutes, or until tender.
2. Add tomato, salt, black and red pepper, and cook 5 more minutes. Add spinach and ¼ cup water. Turn heat to low, and cover pan. Simmer 5 minutes, until spinach is wilted.
3. Remove a little liquid from pan, and stir into peanut butter. Add peanut butter to pan. Simmer and stir until sauce is smooth and hot.

Serve with rice.

Serves 4.

* To make peanut butter the African way, remove the shells from ½ cup of fresh peanuts. Roast the peanuts in a frying pan (or on a cookie sheet in the oven), stirring often, until browned. Then cool, and remove the skins. Return peanuts to pan, and cover partially with water. Bring to a boil, and then simmer on low heat, stirring often, to soften. Crush peanuts with a potato masher.

THE ECONOMY

With ample natural resources, Congo has the potential to become one of Africa's most prosperous nations. But corruption, neglect, and social and political chaos in Congo have damaged the nation's economy since independence in 1960. The Second Congo War, beginning in 1998, severely worsened conditions. Congolese rebels and invading foreign armies illegally exploited the country's diamonds, gold, timber, and other resources. By 2001 the average yearly income had fallen to $100 per person. Economic growth had sunk lower than -6 percent. Inflation had climbed to 630 percent.

Peace and social reforms after 2003 began to turn the economy around. Foreign aid increased. Inflation gradually fell to 26 percent, and growth increased to 7 percent. Still, Congo's average income per person is only $720 annually, and most people live in extreme poverty.

The poor state of Congo's infrastructure—public works such as electricity and water delivery systems—hampers the economy's recovery. Once an exporter of food, Congo must import food to meet the

needs of its citizens. Millions of Congolese do not have enough food and suffer from malnutrition. Many go without basic items such as soap, salt, and shoes.

The nation also struggles with one of the world's largest debts. After 1960 Congo's government borrowed money from international lenders to build energy plants, roads, and other major projects. Corrupt officials pocketed much of the money instead. The nation remains burdened with a debt of more than $10 billion.

The government elected in 2006 promised to establish open and fair economic policies. These and other reforms encourage more foreign investment. A more organized use of Congo's mineral and agricultural resources is expected to improve business and economic options.

It is difficult to assess Congo's economic life accurately. Much business happens outside the formal economy. For instance, rural people often rely on bartering, or swapping goods, rather than using cash. In big cities, many people earn a living through unofficial street

A young woman carries a stalk of sugarcane from a field in northern Congo. She carries her baby in a sling on her back.

businesses. The illegal trade in minerals and other unofficial trading also continues to thrive.

◉ Agriculture

Agriculture—including farming, fishing, and forestry—makes up approximately 55 percent of Congo's gross domestic product (GDP), or the amount of money a country earns in a year. Experts estimate that at least 65 percent of Congo's workforce are farmers. Most of them are subsistence farmers. They are able to grow just enough to feed their families and have no surplus food to sell.

The major crops farmers grow to eat are cassava, plantains, corn, peanuts (called groundnuts in Africa), and rice. The cooler temperatures and fertile soil of the Eastern Highlands favor the cultivation of cabbages, onions, tomatoes, and strawberries. The main tropical fruits are bananas, papayas, mangoes, pineapples, and oranges.

Farmers grow cash crops mostly on large farms, or plantations. These crops, grown to sell, include coffee, palm oil, rubber, sugarcane, tea, cotton, and cocoa.

Cassava is an easy crop to grow. Farmers simply bury a 3-inch (7 cm) piece and wait for it to sprout. Cassava's roots can survive fire and dry seasons. The plant may look dead, but when rain comes, its roots sprout again.

Because the tsetse fly transmits the deadly sleeping sickness disease to cattle, few farmers raise these animals in Congo. Most cattle live in the Southern Uplands and in the Eastern Highlands, where the insect cannot survive. On ordinary farms, common livestock includes goats, pigs, sheep, chickens, ducks, and geese. Hunting wild animals provides the Congolese with more meat than all the domestic livestock combined.

Fishing and Forestry

Fishing is not a key money earner in Congo, but it is an important source of food. Some villagers cooperate to set up elaborate fishing nets across rivers. The lakes in eastern and southern Congo supply freshwater species, such as tilapia. Kisangani is one of the nation's major fishing ports. Farmers also raise fish on fish farms.

Congo exploits only a small fraction of its forests' logging potential. As with the nation's other economic areas, the timber sector suffers from lack of transportation and equipment. Rebels in eastern territories illegally fell timber and sell it across the border. Since 2003 the government has worked to increase logging. Environmental groups are concerned that this increase of up to 60 percent will lead to deforestation. Therefore, the government announced a plan to reforest heavily logged areas.

Services

The service sector offers public and private services rather than the production of goods. It includes jobs in government, transportation, communications, health care, education, retail trade, and tourism. Services provide Congo with about 34 percent of its GDP.

The government is Congo's largest service employer. It spends almost 22 percent of its budget on the armed forces. It also employs teachers and other government workers.

The World Bank, a United Nations agency, conducts a worldwide survey on how challenging it is to do business in various countries. In 2007 the bank ranked Congo as the most difficult place to do business, out of 175 countries. The nation's lack of roads is one of the main difficulties businesses face.

Congo's wealth of natural beauty and wildlife make tourism an area of potential economic growth. Due to security concerns, poor transportation, and lack of guest amenities, such as hotels, only 103,000 foreigners visit the country yearly. They contribute about $2 million to the economy. Most visitors come from other African countries.

Transportation and Communications

The Congo River and its branches are the backbone of Congo's transportation system. Boats run regularly between Kinshasa and Kisangani. Canoelike pirogues commonly carry passengers and goods.

Large commercial boats can navigate 9,062 miles (14,584 km) of Congo's rivers. Shippers and travelers depend on roads and railways to bypass rough sections and waterfalls. Matadi is the main Atlantic port for seagoing vessels. Lakes are important transportation routes to points along Congo's eastern border.

Wars severely damaged the 3,211 miles (5,168 km) of Congo's rail tracks. Railroads nonetheless are vital for moving goods and raw materials across the country. The longest railroad network ties southern Katanga to the port of Ilebo on the Kasai River and on to Kinshasa.

Less than 1,746 miles (2,810 km) of paved roads serve Congo. Heavy rains every year leave Congo's 94,189 miles (151,583 km) of unpaved roads rutted and impassable. International lenders provide funds to improve on the rural road network.

With so few roads in such a large country, air travel is important. Most business travelers save time by flying on Congo Airlines, the state-owned national airline. The main international airport is Ndjili Airport at Kinshasa. Other large airports with paved runways serve Kinshasa, Lubumbashi, and Kisangani. Congo has 209 unpaved airfields.

Few Congolese own cars. Gasoline is scarce and expensive. Most people walk or bicycle where they need to go. Private trucks, taxis, and mini-

Bicyclists walk their overloaded vehicles around a washed-out road north of Goma. The road is the main supply route for northeastern towns.

Congo has the highest ratio of cell to landline users in the world. This Kinshasa **mobile phone store** also sells calls by the minute for those without phones.

buses provide public transportation for city dwellers. Buses are the most common mode of public transportation in Congo's interior. Before setting off, drivers pack the vehicles to overflowing with riders and goods.

Congo's inadequate telecommunications system reflects the country's general lack of public works, such as phone poles and power lines. The country counts only about eleven thousand landline telephones. Cell phones are much more efficient, and 2.7 million Congolese use them.

Radios serve rural areas better than televisions, which require electrical lines. The nation's more than 18 million radios outnumber televisions 3 to 1. Radios broadcast messages to areas where there are no telephones. Congo has one Internet service provider, which serves about 150,000 Internet users. Cybercafes offer public Internet use for a fee in Kinshasa.

Industry and Manufacturing

Congo's poorly developed industrial sector accounts for 11 percent of its GDP. The sector includes manufacturing and mining. Kinshasa and Lubumbashi are the main manufacturing centers. Modern factories are able to manufacture roughly half of what they produced in 1960. Congolese workers produce processed foods such as sugar and flour, beverages (including beer), and more than 3 million cartons of cigarettes. Textiles, printed fabrics, and shoes are other important products. Manufactured cement and other building materials supply the construction trades. Transportation equipment includes tires and bicycles. Industries also specialize in ship repair.

Poor management and shortages of raw materials, such as steel and iron, keep Congo's industrial output low. In addition, a lack of spare parts prevents most factories from running at full capacity. The government attempts to improve the situation by offering tax breaks to foreign companies that will build and operate manufacturing facilities in Congo. Even when goods are produced, however, difficulty transporting them limits the manufacturing sector.

Mining and Trade

Since 2006 renewed mining activity has boosted Congo's economy. Mining provides more than 80 percent of Congo's exports. Diamonds are Congo's leading export earners. The country is the world's fourth-leading diamond producer. The diamond industry provides work for almost one million people. Many miners earn less than one dollar a day, however, and work in dangerous conditions.

Due to high world prices, oil is Congo's second-largest export earner, after diamonds. Congo mines petroleum (oil) offshore, on the Atlantic coast, near the mouth of the Congo River. Foreign oil companies develop and operate most of the oil fields. Because Congo does not have the heavy equipment to refine its oil, it relies on imported fuel.

The southeastern and eastern parts of Congo are the country's mining centers. Copper is found in a 60-mile-wide (96 km) belt in Katanga. Congo is the seventh-largest producer of the metal and supplies about 7 percent of the world's total output. Katanga also has large amounts of cobalt, zinc, and manganese, along with smaller supplies of gold, silver, cadmium, tin, and coal. Sites in Kivu yield tin, tungsten, and gold. Northeastern Congo is also a key source of gold.

Congo holds about 80 percent of the world's columbite-tantalite, or coltan. Changes in world technology in the late 1990s made coltan a big earner for Congo. Cell phone makers require the mineral to create capacitators (special devices that conduct energy).

Congo's main trade exports are diamonds, crude (unrefined) oil, copper, coffee, and cobalt. Congo also sells timber, rubber, cacao (the source of chocolate), tea, cotton, and sugarcane to other countries. Belgium is Congo's most important export partner, followed by the United States, China, France, and Finland.

Visit www.vgsbooks.com for links to websites with additional information about Congo's economy. Read about businesses in Congo, and learn about the diamond trade. Follow the country's efforts to stabilize its economy and improve living conditions for its people.

Congo imports more goods than it exports. Its main imports are consumer goods, food, machinery for mining and transportation, and fuels. Congo buys 18 percent of its imports from South Africa. Belgium, France, Zambia, and Kenya are other major import partners.

Energy

Congo's rivers give the nation the capacity to produce more hydroelectricity (power from water) than any other African country except Cameroon. The Inga hydroelectric station at Inga Falls harnesses the power of rushing water near the mouth of the Congo River, 25 miles (40 km) upstream from the port at Matadi. It is the largest hydropower plant in Africa. A high-voltage transmission line carries the power across the country. It reaches from Inga to the heart of the Katanga's mining region. Smaller hydroelectrical sites on local rivers also serve Katanga.

Mining and other industrial operations consume more than three-quarters of Congo's total electrical output. Residential use is very limited, since less than 2 percent of the population have access to electricity.

The Future

Poverty and instability have long wracked Congo and limited its growth. War destroyed much of the country's infrastructure and disrupted farming and trade. Peace in 2003 offered the chance to reform the economy, return to democracy, and protect human rights. The government elected in 2006 faces the challenge of providing adequate food, clean water, schools, and health care to its citizens. To achieve this, it needs to run fairly and efficiently. Lawlessness and human rights abuses continue to hamper Congo's progress, however.

In 1960, when Congo became independent, its many ethnic groups had no strong sense of nationhood. The Congolese people have since gained a sense of national identity, through the hard times they have endured. Despite some divisions, most Congolese strongly desire one unified, peaceful, and democratic nation.

SIGN OF HOPE

Since the 1960s, Congo's banking system barely worked. People had to buy everything—even cars—with cash. Anyone who had extra money usually hid it at home. The return of democracy offers hope of change. In 2007 a German bank installed Congo's first automated teller machines (ATMs) for electronic banking in Kinshasa. Many people in the capital city welcome the money machines as a rare sign of progress in their country.

8000 B.C. The first people in Congo establish hunting and gathering communities in the rain forest. They are the ancestors of the Mbuti people.

1000 B.C. Bantu-language speakers begin to move into Congo from western Africa. By A.D. 800, they have spread throughout Congo.

A.D. 1400 Different ethnic groups from the north begin to settle in northern Congo. The large Bantu kingdoms of the Kongo, the Luba, the Lunda, and the Kuba begin to form in western and southern Congo.

MID-1400S The Kongo kingdom has grown to cover parts of present-day Angola and the Republic of Congo. Under the skilled leadership of Lopwe kings, the Luba kingdom emerges, between the Kasai River and Lake Tanganyika.

1482 Portuguese trader Diogo Cão arrives at the mouth of the Congo River.

1507 Afonso I (Nzinga Mbemba) becomes Kongo's king. He installs European and Catholic practices in his realm. In this era, plantation owners in the Americas begin to look to Africa as a source of slave labor.

1568 King Alvaro I of Kongo requests Portugal's help in protecting the capital, Mbanzakongo. To repay Portugal, Alvaro allows slave trading to increase.

1620S Shamba Bolongongo becomes king of Kuba. He encourages invention and excellence in art, farming, and building in his thriving kingdom.

1665 Portuguese-held Angola defeats Kongo, marking the decline of the kingdom and further expansion of the slave trade.

1700S Other kingdoms take over the slave trade from Kongo. The Lunda realm expands. Europeans build ports on the African coasts to handle the large numbers of slaves.

1850S Arab African slave trader Tippu Tib sets up his own state on the Lualaba River.

1874 Henry M. Stanley begins his three-year journey down the Congo River, which will attract the attention of King Leopold II of Belgium.

1884 European nations hold the Berlin Conference to discuss dividing Africa into colonies. The next year, they recognize the Congo Free State as Leopold II's private property.

1890 European writer Joseph Conrad works in the Congo Free State, which will be the subject of his famous short novel *Heart of Darkness*. African American journalist George Washington Williams reports about colonial abuse he sees in Congo.

1908 The Belgian parliament makes the Congo Free State a colony called the Belgian Congo. By this time, about 8 million Congolese have died under harsh conditions.

1914 World War I begins. Congolese troops fight German forces in Africa, and Belgian Congo's exports help to pay for the Belgian government in exile during the war.

1940   Germany occupies Belgium during World War II. Congo sup-
        plies soldiers and minerals to the fight against Germany and
        its allies.

1950s   The Alliance of the Kongo People (ABAKO) demands that the colonial
        government provide civil rights.

1960   The Democratic Republic of Congo gains its independence on June 30. The first
        Congo crisis begins when Katanga secedes from the republic.

1061   Rivals execute Prime Minister Lumumba in January in Katanga. The UN forces
        Katanga and other regions to rejoin the Congo republic.

1965   Army leader Joseph-Désiré Mobutu overthrows President Kasa-Vubu.

1970   Mobutu wins presidential elections and consolidates his power as dictator. The
        Kimbanguist church joins the World Council of Churches.

1971   Mobutu begins Africanization. He takes the name Mobutu Sese Seko and changes
        Congo's name to Zaire.

1988   Zaire's government census counts 34.7 million people. About this time, foreign lenders
        accuse Mobutu of keeping for himself the money they loaned to Zaire.

1992   HIV/AIDS infects more than 11,000 people in Zaire.

1994   Refugees from ethnic slaughter in Rwanda create tension in Zaire.

1996   The First Congo War starts. Laurent Kabila leads the anti-Mobutu rebels.

1997   Mobutu goes into exile and President Kabila establishes a government, ending the First
        Congo War. The country takes back the name of Democratic Republic of Congo.

1998   The Second Congo War starts in August. Warring groups terrorize civilians.

2001   An assassin shoots President Kabila to death. His son Joseph Kabila takes over the
        presidency. Congo's average yearly income is $100 per person. The civil war continues.

2002   Volcanic Mount Nyiragongo erupts. The government and the main rebel groups sign a
        peace agreement.

2005   Rebels in the northeast murder nine UN peacekeepers. Voters approve a new con-
        stitution. Tabu Ley becomes vice-governor of Kinshasa.

2006   Voters elect Joseph Kabila as president in Congo's first democratic elections
        since independence. Mining of diamonds, oil, and copper boosts Congo's econ-
        omy.

2007   HIV/AIDS has infected 3.2 percent of the adult population. The UN peace-
        keeping force in Congo remains the largest in the world.

Fast Facts

Currency

COUNTRY NAME Democratic Republic of Congo

AREA 905,063 square miles (2,344,102 sq. km)

MAIN LANDFORMS Congo Basin, Northern Uplands, Southern Uplands, Eastern Highlands, Great Rift Valley, Ruwenzori Mountains, Virunga Mountains

HIGHEST POINT Margherita Peak on Mount Ngaliema (also called Mount Stanley), 16,762 feet (5,110 m)

LOWEST POINT Atlantic Ocean, sea level

MAJOR RIVERS Congo, Lualaba, Kasai, Tshuapa, and Ubangi

ANIMALS antelopes, baboons, black-and-white colobuses, bonobos, buffalo, chimpanzees, eland, elephants, hippopotamuses, hyenas, jackals, leopards, lions, monkeys, mountain gorillas, okapi, rhinoceroses, zebras; cranes, eagles, honeyguides, parrots, partridges, storks, sunbirds, weavers; capitaine (Nile perch), dolphins, eels, electric catfish, jellyfish; crocodiles, frogs, lizards, pythons, salamanders, tree cobras, turtles, vipers

CAPITAL CITY Kinshasa

OTHER MAJOR CITIES Lubumbashi, Kananga, Kisangani

OFFICIAL LANGUAGES French, Lingala, Kiswahili, Kikongo, and Tshiluba

MONETARY UNIT 1 Congolese franc = 100 centimes

CURRENCY

The Congolese franc replaced the former zaire as Congo's unit of currency in 1998. Coins are not used. Congo's banknotes (paper bills) are issued in denominations of 1, 5, 10, 20, and 50 centimes, and 1, 5, 10, 20, 50, and 100 francs. In 2000, 200-franc notes were introduced, followed by 500-franc notes in 2002. Banknotes depict different scenes of Congo's culture, environment, and economy. Illustrations include a Chokwe mask, elephants and lions, a fishing village, and a river dam.

U.S. currency is also widely accepted in Congo. Most vendors and banks accept only U.S. banknotes made in 1996 or after, because their off-center portraits are harder to counterfeit.

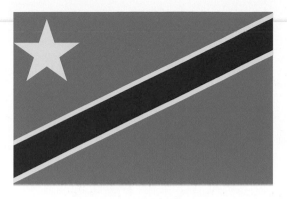

Congo has had several flags. The country flew a blue and yellow flag at its 1960 independence. From 1963 to 1997, other flags represented the country. A new government reintroduced the first flag in 1997. In 2006 a new constitution came into effect, and the nation adopted yet another flag. The background color of the 2006 flag is sky blue. A red stripe bordered by two narrow yellow lines runs from the flag's lower left corner to the upper right corner. In the upper left corner appears a yellow star with five points.

"Debout Congolaise" (Arise Congolese) is the national anthem of Congo. The country chose the song at independence in 1960. President Mobutu changed the anthem in 1972. Laurent Kabila restored it in 1997. Joseph Lutumba wrote the song's words, in French. S. Boka di Mpasi Londi wrote the music. The words *thirtieth June* refer to the date of independence.

ENGLISH TRANSLATION

Arise, Congolese, united by fate,
United in the struggle for independence,
Let us hold up our heads, so long bowed,
And now, for good, let us keep moving boldly ahead, in peace.
Oh, ardent people, by hard work we shall build,
In peace, a country more beautiful than before.

Countrymen, sing the sacred hymn of your solidarity,
Proudly salute the golden emblem of your sovereignty, Congo.

REFRAIN
Note: The choir sings the words in parentheses. A soloist sings the rest.

Blessed gift (Congo) of our forefathers (Congo),
Oh (Congo) beloved country (Congo),
We shall people your soil and ensure your greatness.
(Thirtieth June) Oh gentle sun (thirtieth June) of thirtieth June,
(Sacred day) Be witness (sacred day) of the immortal oath of freedom
That we hand on to our children forever.

 Visit www.vgsbooks.com for a link to a website where you can listen to Congo's national anthem, "Debout Congolaise."

In some cases, accurate information about birth and death dates for Congolese people is not available. Dates have been listed below, where known.

SERGE DIKULU BAGETA (b. 1978) Soccer star Bageta was born in Kinshasa. He played for two Congo teams before joining the South African team Ajax Cape Town in 2003. Bageta plays a key role in the Ajax's defense.

AMBA BONGO Born in Kinshasa, Bongo lives in London, England. She is a writer and a champion for human rights, especially for refugees. Bongo worked in the ministry of education in Congo. She fled in 1991 because she suffered persecution after having spoken out against her corrupt bosses. Her novel *Une femme en exil* (A Woman in Exile) came out in 2000, followed by *Cécilia*. She is the project director for Active Women, which helps French-speaking African women in the United Kingdom. Bongo's website is http://www.ambabongo.com/ambaenglish.htm.

HONORATA Honorata's story represents the experience of many Congolese women during the Second Congo War and afterward. Born in eastern Congo, she became well known after American talk-show host Oprah Winfrey featured her story of survival in 2005. Honorata relates that in 2002, armed rebels captured, raped, and tortured her. She escaped and walked more than 150 miles (240 km) to Bukavu, a village with many people fleeing the war. There she found her five children, and they began to rebuild their life together. Honorata joined a program for women displaced by war, sponsored by Women for Women International, in 2004. She learned basic job skills and started a small business. On International Women's Day 2004, she gave a speech, calling on national officials and the international community to pay attention to the war crimes women suffer in Congo. Life remains a struggle, but Honorata is determined to have a house where she and her family can live in peace.

JOSEPH KABILA (b. 1971) In 2006 Kabila became the first democratically elected president of Congo since independence. The son of former president Laurent Kabila, Joseph Kabila was born in his father's rebel headquarters in the Fizi territory of South Kivu. He went to college in Uganda before military training in China. In 1996 Kabila joined his father's rebel movement that toppled the dictator Mobutu in 1997. After his father's murder, twenty-nine-year-old Kabila became president on January 17, 2001. He promised to create peace, improve living conditions, and lead the country into full democracy. Unlike his father, he worked with some success to keep these promises. His government and main rebel groups agreed to peace and a power-sharing government in December 2002. Kabila and his wife Olive Lembe di Sita have one daughter, born in 2001.

MONSENGWO KEJWAMFI (1950–2001) The painter, known as Moke, was one of Congo's best-loved artists. He came to Kinshasa as a ten-year-old orphan. The boy supported himself by making paintings on pieces of cardboard. Moke became a painter who recorded Kinshasa's street scenes and human nature with kindness and often humor. He led the Kinshasa-based Popular Painting Movement. Artists in the group used many colorful and fun elements of pop art. They also believed that art can influence history.

SIMUN KIMBANGU (ca. 1889–1951) Kimbangu was born into a poor Kongo family in Nkamba, in the Congo Free State. Baptized a Christian as a teenager, Kimbangu soon began to have spiritual visions that told him to be a healer in the name of Jesus Christ. Kimbangu began to practice faith healing. He preached strict Christianity and rejected traditional African religion. His message greatly appealed to poor, suffering, and powerless people. But the Belgian authorities were afraid he might become a leader for an independence movement. In 1921 the Belgians arrested him and sentenced him to death. European Christian missionaries protested, and the officials changed his sentence to life in prison. Kimbangu died in prison in 1951. His youngest son, Joseph Diangienda, led the church after Congo's independence, and the church joined the World Council of Churches in 1970. Some believers see Simon Kimbangu as an African savior.

MBILIA BEL Born in Congo, Mbilia Bel is the stage name of a singer known as the queen of Congolese rumba, or soukous. She began her musical career when she was seventeen and rose to fame when she joined the Afrisa International band in 1981. She became one of the first female musicians from Africa to gain popularity all over the continent and beyond. The dynamic combination of bandleader Tabu Ley Rochereau and Mbilia Bel resulted in Afrisa records' soaring success. Mbilia Bel's dancing also often added spice to Tabu Ley's already famous live performances. The two performers later married. Mbilia Bel's first song with Afrisa, released in 1982, was "Mpeve Ya Longo," which means "Holy Spirit" in Kikongo. In the song, she sang about a woman raising her children alone after her husband leaves her. The song was a big hit, especially among Congolese women. Mbilia Bel quit the band late in 1987 to pursue a solo career. In her 2004 release *Belissimo*, she blends rap into her familiar style.

ANTOINE KOFFI OLOMIDE (b. 1956) is a musician who sings, produces, and composes music in the soukous, or African rumba, style. Olomide grew up in Kinshasa and attended college in Paris, France. In the 1970s, back in Congo, he reintroduced a slow style of soukous, which he called tcha tcho. Olomide's deep, smooth voice gained popularity worldwide in the 1990s. Olomide also performs fast, hip-swaying dance music called soukous ndombolo. He tours widely with his band and released his twenty-eighth album in 2005.

The U.S. Department of State (http://travel.state.gov/travel/cis_pa_tw/tw/tw_2198.html) warns against travel to Congo because conditions within the country remain dangerous.

KAHUZI-BIEGA NATIONAL PARK is about 19 miles (30 km) from Bukavu and covers an area of about 1.5 million acres (600,000 hectares). The park gets its name from the two highest peaks in the park, Kahuzi and Biega. Its forests are home to elephants, buffalo, antelopes, leopards, mongooses, and more. Many ape and monkey species live in the park. Tours operate in the park during peaceful times, including guided hikes up Mount Kahuzi.

KINSHASA is the capital city and the gateway for travelers to Congo. Once nicknamed Kin La Belle, for "Beautiful Kinshasa" in French, this city lost much of its beauty during many years of turmoil. Historical buildings include a large Roman Catholic cathedral built in 1914. The National Museum of Kinshasa displays the best collection of Congolese art in the country. The Kinshasa University hosts excellent art collections and museums. Modern hotels, shops, and restaurants serve Kinshasa. Craftspeople produce wood and metal items for sale in Kinshasa's markets. Travelers should take extra care at night, but it is fairly safe to experience the lively nightlife in the neighborhood called Zone de Matonge.

LOLA YA BONOBO opened in 1994 near Kinshasa as a sanctuary for bonobos, the great apes unique to Congo. It works with Congo's ministry of environment to rescue live bonobos that are illegally sold for meat in the streets of Kinshasa and cities. More than fifty confiscated or orphaned bonobos live at Lola ya Bonobo, in a forest park. The sanctuary plans to return some to the wild. Lola ya Bonobo runs education programs for urban youth, environmental activists, and other visitors. The sanctuary's website is http://www.friendsofbonobos.org.

MBANZA-NGUNGU in Congo's southwest is a pleasant resort area with a good climate. The Mbanza-Ngungu area offers world-famous rare orchids at the Frère Gillet Botanic Gardens. Visitors to the area also enjoy caves and the Inkisi Falls (197 feet, or 60 meters, high) in the region. Farther east are the wild slopes and gorges of the Kwilu River.

VIRUNGA NATIONAL PARK covers 4,633 square miles (12,000 sq. km). Two jagged mountain ranges border the park and serve as a natural fence for wild animals, which roam free. Game includes antelopes, elephants, lions, and colorful waterbirds. The tourist office at Goma makes arrangements for visitors to see rare mountain gorillas in the park and to hike in the mountains and up to volcanic craters. In 2007, the park began rebuilding the trail that leads up Mount Ruwenzori, a major attraction for climbers. The parkland stretches into Uganda and Rwanda and includes the craters of volcanoes Nyiragongo and Nyamulagira.

animism: a religious practice of spirit worship. Practitioners believe spirit (conscious life) inhabits all living and nonliving natural objects, natural events (such as lightning), and human ancestors.

Bantu: a family of languages spoken in central and southern Africa, or a member of any group of African people who speak one of these languages. *Bantu* means "people."

canopy: the top level of a rain forest, where tree branches form a continuous, interlocking web of leaves to capture sunlight

colony: a territory controlled by a foreign power and partially inhabited by settlers from that foreign land

coup: the sudden overthrow of a government

dictator: a leader who rules with absolute power, often through oppressive and violent means

equator: an imaginary circle around Earth that is halfway between the North Pole and the South Pole. The equator divides the Northern Hemisphere and the Southern Hemisphere. The climate near the equator is the hottest on Earth.

gross domestic product (GDP): the value of the goods and services produced by a country over a period of time, usually one year

ivory: the creamy white substance that makes up elephants' tusks

literacy: the ability to read and write a basic sentence

poaching: the catching or killing of animals illegally

polygyny: the practice of a husband having more than one wife at once, common in traditional sub-Saharan African societies

soukous: Congolese guitar-driven dance music, popular throughout Africa, also known as Congo or African rumba

subsistence farmers: farmers able to grow just enough to feed their families, with no surplus food left over to sell

tropical rain forest: a warm, humid, and thick woodland that lies in regions near the equator. Tropical rain forests receive at least 80 inches (203 cm) of rain per year and often much more.

the West: non-Communist nations west of Asia, including Belgium and the United States

Africa South of the Sahara. **London, UK: Routledge, 2007.**
This volume is part of the annual Europa Regional Surveys of the World series. Its long, in-depth article on Congo covers Congo's recent history, economy, and government. It also offers a wealth of statistics on population, employment, trade, and more. A short directory of offices and organizations is included.

Belgian Parliament. "Belgian Parliamentary Committee's Conclusion." 2001.
http://www.lachambre.be/kvvcr/pdf_sections/comm/lmb/conclusions.pdf (July 2007).
In 2001 a Belgian legislative committee examined the role of the Belgian government in the murder of Prime Minister Lumumba in 1961. This report of their findings concludes that "certain members of the Belgian government and other Belgian participants were morally responsible for the circumstances leading to the death of Lumumba."

British Broadcasting Corporation. "Country Profile: Democratic Republic of Congo." *BBC News.* **2007.**
http://news.bbc.co.uk/2/hi/africa/country_profiles/1076399.stm (July 2007).
This website includes a country profile of Congo, as well as links to news and information about Africa and the world.

Central Intelligence Agency. "The World Factbook–Congo, Democratic Republic of The." *The World Factbook.* **2007.**
http://www.cia.gov/cia/publications/factbook/geos/cg.html (July 2007).
The U.S. CIA provides this general profile of Congo. The profile includes brief summaries of the nation's geography, people, government, economy, communications, transportation, and military.

Conrad, Joseph. *Heart of Darkness.* **New York: Everyman's Library, 1993.**
Conrad based this famous short novel on his six months in the Congo Free State in 1890. First published in 1902, it relates the journey of a European named Marlow on the Congo River. Among much brutality, Marlow finds the "heart of darkness" in a white man who has become insane in his greed and lives in a house surrounded by human heads on stakes. Filmmaker Francis Ford Coppola based his 1979 film about U.S. soldiers in Vietnam, *Apocalypse Now*, partly on this book.

Federal Research Division, Library of Congress. *A Country Study: Congo (Former).* **Washington, DC: Federal Research Division, Library of Congress, 1993.**
http://lcweb2.loc.gov/ frd/cs/zrtoc.html#zr0006 (July 2007).
This thorough study of Congo includes extensive coverage of its history up to 1993 (when it was still Zaire).

Hochschild, Adam. *King Leopold's Ghost: A Story of Greed, Terror, and Heroism in Colonial Africa.* **Boston: Houghton Mifflin, 1998.**
In this book, the author explores different angles of King Leopold's Congo Free State. He explains how the Belgian king came to own the land in the 1880s and the brutal exploitation that followed. He also presents the Africans who resisted and the Westerners who worked for reforms.

IRIN. "North-Kivu, DRC: Living on the Fringes of Society: What Future for Young Ex-Combatants?" IRIN. February 23, 2007.
http://www.irinnews.org/Report.aspx?ReportId=69991 (August 2007).
This article on Congo's child soldiers is part of a series examining how conflict, poverty, and alienation affect the lives of children and teens. The article looks at the lives of Congolese children who lost years of their childhood to being part of a militia group. They continue to struggle daily to survive in an environment where they cannot count on safety or belonging.

Lumumba, Patrice. "Lumumba's Last Letter." *Africa Within*. (N.d.)
http://www.africawithin.com/lumumba/last_letter.htm (July 2007).
This is the full text of Lumumba's last letter, written to his wife shortly before his assassination in January 1961. The letter opens: "I write you these words without knowing . . . if I will still be living when you read them."

Maurer, Evan M., and Niangi Batulukisi. *Spirits Embodied: Art of the Congo*. Minneapolis: Minneapolis Institute of Arts, 1999.
This book was produced to go along with an exhibition of the same name. Informative text accompanies the many color photographs.

PRB. "PRB 2007 World Population Data Sheet." *Population Reference Bureau*. 2007.
http://www.prb.org (July 2007).
This annual statistics sheet provides a wealth of population, demographic, and health statistics for Congo and almost all countries in the world.

Robarts, Fred. "Chéri Samba: Interview." *Time Out London*, March 28, 2007.
http://www.timeout.com/london/art/features/2760.html (July 2007).
Time Out, a London news magazine, interviewed Samba, one of Congo's best-known artists. Samba explains that he considers himself a painter-journalist, inspired by daily life "to represent things as they are, to communicate with humour, to ask relevant questions and to tell the truth."

***The Statesman's Yearbook: The Politics, Cultures, and Economics of the World, 2007*. New York: St. Martin's Press, 2006.**
This annual publication provides concise information on Congo's history, climate, government, economy, and culture, including relevant statistics.

U.S. Department of State, Bureau of African Affairs. "Background Note: Democratic Republic of the Congo." *U.S. Department of State*. 2007.
http://www.state.gov/r/pa/ei/bgn/2823.htm (March 2007).
This website provides a general profiles of Congo's geography, people, government and politics, and economy, produced by the U.S. Department of State.

Women for Women International. "Stories from the Front: Honorata." *Womenforwomen.org*. 2007.
http://www.womenforwomen.org/sfcongo.htm#Honorata (August 2007).
Women for Women International supports programs to help women in conflict or war and postwar situations. This page of the organization's larger website tells the story of Honorata, who survived capture at the hands of a rebel army in eastern Congo and went on to rebuild her life.

Africa Studies Center. University of Pennsylvania. Democratic Republic of Congo Page
http://www.africa.upenn.edu/Country_Specific/Zaire.html
This site provides links to a wide variety of online resources about Congo. Topics include diamonds, human rights, languages, and much more.

Buettner, Dan. *Africatrek: A Journey by Bicycle through Africa.* Minneapolis: Lerner Publications Company, 1997.
Minnesotan Buettner and four other team members biked 11,855 miles (18,968 km) across Africa. The hardest part of their trip was through Zaire (Congo). They faced rutted mud roads, suffocating rain forests, illness, and heavily armed soldiers who demanded bribes. Luckily, they also met people who helped them. The author's photographs accompany this tale of adventure.

Culturebase.net. "Bodys Isek Kingelez."
http://www.culturebase.net/artist.php?210
View some of artist Bodys Isek Kingelez's fantastic architectural models on this site. The site also hosts works by other Congolese artists.

Diouf, Sylviane Anna. *Kings and Queens of Central Africa.* New York: Franklin Watts, 2000.
Africa has a history of strong leaders who united different peoples into nations. This book for younger readers presents Congo rulers Afonso I, king of the Kongo, and Shamba Bolongongo, king of the Bakuba (or Kuba).

Go Congo
http://www.gocongo.com/gc2home/gchome.html
With Congo mostly at peace, tourists can visit parts of this magnificent country again. Go Congo Tour Operators offer information and links about trips to Congo for adventurous travelers on this site.

Green, Jen. *Rain Forest.* New York: DK Publishing, 2004.
Colorful graphics and see-through overlays in this book give the reader an unusual view of life in the world's rain forests.

Heale, Jay. *Democratic Republic of the Congo.* New York: Marshall Cavendish, 1999.
This book for younger readers offers an introduction to the geography, history, government, economy, people, and culture of Congo.

Jenike, David, and Mark Jenike. *A Walk through a Rain Forest: Life in the Ituri Forest of Zaire.* New York: Franklin Watts, 1994.
Congo's Ituri Forest is one of the most diverse places on Earth. The authors present the rain forests animals, plants, and people in vivid color photographs and fascinating text.

Kingsolver, Barbara. *The Poisonwood Bible.* New York: HarperCollins, 1999.
This best-selling novel follows a Christian missionary family from the United States living in the Belgian Congo in the months shortly before liberation in 1960. It follows each member through the following thirty years, showing through their eyes the history of Congo and the ways in which American and African cultures collide.

Okeke, Chika. *Kongo*. New York: Rosen, 1997.
This Heritage Library of African Peoples title presents to younger readers the land, societies, and history of Congo's ethnic groups. Other titles in the series that cover Congo's people are: *Kuba*, by Rebecca Leuchak; *Luba*, by Mary Rooter Roberts and Allen F. Roberts; and *Mbuti* by Onukaba A. Ojo.

Tayler, Jeffrey. *Facing the Congo*. Saint Paul: Ruminator Books, 2000.
American travel writer Tayler writes of his journey on the Congo River in this fascinating book. Taking a crowded barge upriver in 1995, when Mobutu's military still gripped Zaire, Tayler returned downriver in a canoelike pirogue.

Twist, Clint. *Stanley and Livingstone: Expeditions through Africa*. Austin, TX: Raintree Steck-Vaughn, 1995.
Henry M. Stanley's explorations in Congo in the nineteenth century opened the land for European exploitation. This book for younger readers presents Stanley and David Livingstone, his fellow explorer of Africa.

vgsbooks.com
http://www.vgsbooks.com
Visit vgsbooks.com, the homepage of the Visual Geography Series®, which is updated regularly. You can get linked to all sorts of useful online information, including geographical, historical demographic, cultural, and economic websites. The vgsbooks.com site is a great resource for late-breaking news and statistics.

***When We Were Kings*. DVD. Directed by Leon Gast. Produced by DAS Films, David Sonenberg Production. London: Polygram Filmed Entertainment, 1997.**
This documentary follows the 1974 championship boxing fight in Kinshasa, Congo. The contenders were Americans George Foreman, the reigning champion, and underdog challenger Muhammad Ali.

Wildlife Direct Blogs
www.http://wildlifedirect.org/
This site links to Congo park rangers' blogs. The rangers work to protect wildlife and habitats in difficult, isolated, and often dangerous conditions. Their blogs offer fascinating glimpses of day-to-day life in Congo's wildlife reserves.

Willis, Terri. *Democratic Republic of the Congo*. New York: Children's Press, 2004.
Part of the Enchantment of the World series, this book for younger readers describes the geography, history, culture, industry, and people of Congo.

Yamusangie, Frederick K.
http://www.frederickyamusangie.org.uk/
The is the homepage of Congolese author Yamusangie, who lives in the United Kingdom. A link leads to the first two chapters of his book *Full Circle* (2003), about a Congolese boy. The novel is published by iUniverse.

Captions for photos appearing on cover and chapter openers:

Cover: Men from the fishing village of Wagenia, near Kisangani, use handmade nets to harvest fish from the Congo River.

pp. 4–5 Forests cover the rugged hills of Virunga National Park. The park includes some of Congo's most stunning terrain, including volcanoes, marshes, and savannas.

pp. 8–9 Terraced fields cover a fertile valley near Lake Kivu.

pp. 20–21 Traditional mud brick homes with thatched roofs sit on the edge of a Congo banana plantation north of Bukavu.

pp. 40–41 Travelers in Katanga Province carry their belongings in bundles on their heads.

pp. 48–49 Children play brass instruments in a local band. They live near the border of Uganda.

pp. 58–59 Boys, some as young as eight years old, dig copper in a mine near Lubumbashi.